I'll Bring My Own Chair

THE LIFE OF ADRIAN BATTCOCK

Eleanor Dawson
with Jeanine Battcock

BREAKWATER BOOKS LIMITED
www.breakwaterbooks.com
P O Box 2188 · St. John's · NL · Canada · A1C 6E6

CERTIFIED CANADIAN PUBLISHER

LIBRARY AND ARCHIVES CANADA CATALOGUING IN PUBLICATION

Title: I'll bring my own chair : the incredible life of Adrian Battcock / Eleanor Dawson with Jeanine Battcock.
Other titles: I will bring my own chair
Names: Dawson, Eleanor (Of Newfoundland), author. | Battcock, Jeanine, author.
Identifiers: Canadiana (print) 2026021678X | Canadiana (ebook) 20260216801 | ISBN 9781778530968 (softcover) | ISBN 9781778530975 (EPUB)
Subjects: LCSH: Battcock, Adrian. | LCSH: Lawyers—Canada—Biography. | LCSH: People with quadriplegia—Canada—Biography. | LCGFT: Biographies.
Classification: LCC KE416.B348 D39 2026 | LCC KF345.Z9 B348 2026 kfmod | DDC 340.092—dc23

DESIGN John van der Woude, JVDW Designs
COVER PHOTO Adrian Battcock with Chief Justice Arthur Mifflin, credit Myrna Kielley Photo Service, St. John's
AUTHOR PHOTO Monica Walsh (Eleanor Dawson) and Excu Head Shots (Jeanine Battcock)

THE PUBLISHER GRATEFULLY ACKNOWLEDGES THE SUPPORT OF
The Canada Council for the Arts;
The Government of Canada through the Department of Heritage; and
The Government of Newfoundland and Labrador through the Department of Tourism, Culture, Arts and Recreation

Canada Council for the Arts | Conseil des Arts du Canada | Canada | Newfoundland Labrador

PRINTED AND BOUND IN CANADA

Breakwater Books is committed to choosing papers and materials for our books that help to protect our environment. To this end, this book is made of certified and other controlled material.

FSC www.fsc.org MIX Paper | Supporting responsible forestry FSC® C103567

Contents

A Note and Acknowledgements xi

1. A Life Changed 1
2. The Early Years 4
3. Uncle Henry 12
4. The School Years: Mount Cashel 16
5. Visits Home 31
6. Returning to Mount Cashel 38
7. Life After Mount Cashel 41
8. The DEW Line 48
9. Working with the United Nations 52
10. Returning to Newfoundland 63
11. The Accident 71
12. Moving to the Hoyles Home 79
13. University Life 86
14. A Special Friend 93
15. Moving to Halifax 98
16. Returning to St. John's 105
17. Life at the Department of Justice 109

18. A Special Mentor 114
19. Disability Rights Movement 116
20. Community Services Council 120
21. The Building Accessibility Act 125
22. The Independent Living Resource Centre 130
23. Wheelchair Accessible Bus Service and The HUB 134
24. Coalition of Persons with Disabilities (COD) 138
25. Personal Time 146
26. National Advisory Commission of Employment Equity 153
27. The Hoyles Home in the 1980s & 1990s 160
28. Criminal Injuries Compensation Board 167
29. A Special Protégé 172
30. The End 175

A Note and Acknowledgements

from JEANINE BATTCOCK

Sometimes a dream is just that—something you carry around for years, quietly wondering if you'll ever actually do it…or if it will simply follow you for the rest of your life, tapping you on the shoulder at the most inconvenient times, like a persistent, very polite ghost.

This book was never my dream. It belonged to my darling cousin, Ann Marie Buckingham—an English major at Memorial University of Newfoundland, a beautiful writer, and my very best friend. She was also, it must be said, the one with the vision. I was more the supportive audience, occasionally taking notes in the margins of life.

When *The Other Side of the Mountain* came out in 1973, Ann Marie and I sat side by side crying like little girls as we watched the screen.

That story stayed with Ann Marie. The strength of Jill Kinmont, rebuilding her life after a devastating accident, lit something in Ann Marie.

At the same time, our own family was living through something just as life altering. After a terrible accident, our Uncle

Adrian became a quadriplegic. The very next morning, Ann Marie announced—calmly, confidently, and with absolutely no hesitation—that one day she would write a book about Uncle Adrian. I didn't question it. I just accepted it as fact. When Annie said something like that, it wasn't a dream. It was more like a scheduled future event.

On February 7, 1993, I lost her.

There's no tidy way to describe what comes after that kind of loss. Grief doesn't move in a straight line. It shows up uninvited, lingers longer than you expect, and settles into places you didn't even know existed. For years, I held onto her dream as if it were still somehow within reach. Letting it go felt like losing her a second time.

For a long time, I believed this book would never exist. During those years, my Uncle Adrian became one of my steady places. His sister, Carmel—Ann Marie's mother—was living with a heartbreak no parent should ever have to carry. And yet, through all of it, Carms and I found comfort in each other.

During those years, I often suggested to Adrian that I would attempt to write the book, and he gave his blessing, but only after he was gone. I made the promise and I kept it as I understood the why.

Three members of my family attended Mount Cashel in the 1940s and remembered it with gratitude for the education they received. At the time, it was respected, trusted, and deeply woven into the community. No one imagined what would later come to light.

I remember when the news of abuse finally broke. It felt like the ground shifted under something we had always believed to be solid. As children, we loved driving past the orphanage in St. John's. My father would point out where he had lived, where he and Adrian played sports. His eyes would light up as he told stories—especially the ones about Adrian attempting to run away or skip class, which he apparently treated as a full-time hobby.

When the truth came out, that light dimmed. The stories didn't disappear, but they carried something heavier.

Years later, I asked my father if there was anything he had ever kept hidden. He answered quickly—no—and spoke kindly of the Christian Brothers. That was his experience. But I have never forgotten how different that experience was for so many others. The victims of Mount Cashel are never far from my thoughts. It could have been otherwise. But for God's grace.

When my father, John Battcock, passed away in September 2010, we began clearing out his house. Tucked away were boxes he had saved after Adrian's passing. Inside were hundreds of letters—some from remarkable people—along with scrapbooks, photographs, and pieces of a life carefully preserved. Jack and I looked at it all and made a very quick decision: we were taking everything back to Ontario. Instead of shipping anything, we decided to drive Dad's car back ourselves—filling it with as many boxes as it could possibly hold.

As I began working on this book, I found myself reconnecting with family. One of the greatest gifts was reconnecting with my dear cousin, Mary Margaret Martin Rowe. Mary Margaret is, quite honestly, unforgettable. She is sharp, funny, wonderfully direct, and blessed with the memory of an elephant, in direct contrast to her petite beauty.

She remembers being Adrian's "little buddy," which gave her a front-row seat to many of his adventures—though, for everyone's sake, not all of those adventures are making it into this book. Through her stories, Adrian became fuller to me. Not just someone we loved, but someone who truly lived, laughed, and, I suspect, occasionally caused just enough trouble to keep things interesting.

One of the most delicate decisions in writing this book was how much of Adrian's personal life to include. He was, it must be said, quite popular with women—both before and after the accident. While that was certainly part of his charm, he was also a deeply private and respectful man.

In the end, we chose to leave some things to the reader's imagination. That said, I feel fairly confident in saying that Saturday nights were not always reserved for *Hockey Night in Canada*. Not even close.

At a certain point, it became clear that I could not do this alone. Writing is a lonely process, and running my home-staging business, Newfie Sisters Inc., did not exactly leave long, peaceful stretches of time for reflection and research. Finding the right partner took time, and it was essential that the person be in Newfoundland, familiar to our culture and traditions. As it turns out, the answer came through Mary Margaret, who suggested her cousin, Eleanor Dawson. I'm almost grateful I didn't fully realize how accomplished she was before we first spoke—I might have talked myself out of it. Instead, I simply liked her. Instantly. Eleanor has become not only a trusted collaborator, but a great researcher, with attention to facts, timelines, and organization. We now know she is a gifted writer and this book would not have happened without her. Eleanor has become part of the family and is adored.

And finally, to the people who carried me through all of this:

To my son Mark—thank you for believing in this story and for believing I could tell it, even when I wasn't so sure myself. Thank you for your patience, your help, and for reminding me, again and again, "This is our family. This is who we are."

To Jack—my best friend and constant support—you have stood beside me through everything. You understand me in a way that is both comforting and, at times, a little scary. And somehow, you're still here. I love you for that, and everything in between.

To my sister Michele—thank you for always being ready to jump on a plane to Newfoundland at a moment's notice. No questions asked. You are my sister, my best friend.

To my brother and sister, Johnny and JoAnn, thank you for sharing your memories and being so supportive of my plan from the day I claimed the boxes from Dad's house! Your support means everything.

Lea and Robert—thank you for your encouragement and for being part of my life in all the ways that matter. You are a blessing in my life!

Aunt Sheila and Uncle Bob, your contributions and support have been enormous. Growing up with you in Port aux Basques was a blessing, and our years of separation washed away when this project we started. You both have been instrumental to building Adrian's story and Uncle Bob's memories of Mount Cashel were insightful and important to this story.

To my cousin Keith McGrath, who passed before this book was completed—there is an emptiness in not being able to place this in your hands. Thanks to you and your son Matthew for your continued support.

To my Buckingham cousins and extended family—thank you for your stories, your memories, and your trust.

Darlene, you have been listening to this story for over twenty years. Twenty years. Thank you for the drives, the laughter, and for carrying that heavy tote more times than anyone reasonably should.

To my Newfie Sisters team—Darlene, Linda-Jo, Gus, and the Parris team—thank you for keeping everything running and making me look far more organized than I actually am.

To our editor, Eva Crocker—your insight, humour, and steady guidance made this process not only possible but genuinely enjoyable. Thank you for keeping us on track! You are truly gifted!

And to Rebecca Rose and the team at Breakwater Books—thank you for believing in this story and giving it a home. Being welcomed by you has meant more than I can properly express, and we are eternally grateful.

Adrian's niece, Ann Marie Buckingham. Angels claimed Ann Marie in 1993. It was her dream to write this book; Jeanine loved the idea, and wanted to embrace Ann Marie's dream of writing our uncle's story!

from the AUTHOR

I never imagined that I would write a book. It was my cousin, Mary Martin Rowe, who first suggested me for the project. When Jeanine Battcock approached me, I felt both excited and frightened.

From the beginning, the three of us agreed that we would meet regularly to review my progress and that if it became clear I was floundering, we would stop the project. Instead, those meetings kept the work on track, and gradually the manuscript began to take shape. Through extensive interviews and archival research, I was able to piece together the details of Adrian's life. Although I had never met Adrian personally, I had long been aware of him. We were not related by blood, but shared mutual first cousins: Adrian's Aunt Ella was married to my Uncle Edward, creating a familial connection through marriage.

As a child, I often heard my cousins speak about their cousin Adrian, describing him as exceptionally fun loving and full of life. Years later, while I was a student at Memorial University in the early 1970s, I recognized him on campus. By then, his story was well known at the university, and I would see him in the tunnels, invariably surrounded by other students. His presence was unmistakable; his aura was palpable.

St. John's is a small place, and when I began researching this book, I discovered that many people I knew had also known Adrian. Adrian's sister, Sheila McGrath, and her husband, Robert (Bob) McGrath, became primary sources of information. Coincidentally, I had known them through a previous job, making this a natural starting point for my research. In addition to being Adrian's brother-in-law, Bob McGrath had grown up in Mount Cashel and was able to provide detailed first-hand insight into the institution, how it operated, and what daily life was like there, including his time with Adrian.

Adrian's niece, Jeanine Battcock, had preserved all of Adrian's papers, which she generously made available to me. Other family members also contributed valuable information and perspectives, helping to complete and contextualize the story of Adrian's life. I also interviewed caregivers from the Hoyles Home, where Adrian spent the last twenty-five years of his life. Many of Adrian's friends from his university years, as well as colleagues from his time at the Department of Justice, were generous with their memories and insights. In addition, I consulted archival material related to his various occupations.

Wherever I went in search of information, people were unfailingly helpful. Through these conversations and sources, I came to feel that I knew Adrian intimately, despite never having met him.

There are many people whose support and encouragement made this journey possible, and I am deeply grateful to each of them. First, I want to acknowledge Jeanine Battcock, who entrusted me with this profoundly emotional story—one she had carried with her for many years and held very close to her heart. It was an honour to help bring this story into the world.

I am especially thankful to my cousin, Mary Martin Rowe, for recommending me for this project. Your belief in me opened the door to an experience I will always cherish.

My sincere appreciation goes to our editor, Eva Crocker, whose insight, patience, and thoughtful guidance were invaluable throughout the editing process. Your steady support helped shape this work in meaningful ways. I am also grateful to Breakwater Books for believing in this project and giving it a home.

To my dear friends Bob and Sheila McGrath, thank you for your generosity with your time and energy—spending long hours in conversation and carefully reading multiple drafts of the manuscript. Your feedback and encouragement meant more than I can express.

I would also like to thank Des Walsh and Monica Walsh for their helpful advice in the early stages of editing, as well as Joan Dawson, Jinji Dawson, and Steve Dawson for taking the time to read early versions and offer thoughtful suggestions that strengthened the work.

Also thank you to Emma Butler, Colleen Hanrahan, Libby Creelman, Ron Cole, Paul Dicks, Shawn FitzGerald, Anne Marie Linehan, Lois Martin, Tom Mills, Fergus O'Byrne, Penny Rowe, Brendan Walsh, Don Walsh, and Lynn Sorenson.

To everyone else who contributed in ways both large and small, please know that your support has not gone unnoticed. This project is richer because of you.

ONE

A Life Changed

ON JULY 16, 1966, A DEVASTATING ACCIDENT IN Bay d'Espoir left thirty-one-year-old Adrian Battcock paralyzed from the neck down as the result of a severed spinal cord. At the time, Adrian had been working as a project manager for the Bay d'Espoir Hydroelectric Development, a role he'd held for two years after spending six years with the United Nations' Special Services Division, working across India and Africa.

A temporary bridge on a construction road collapsed under Adrian's vehicle, plunging it into the river below. Though the two other passengers survived with minor injuries, Adrian was initially presumed dead. His rescue and subsequent struggle for survival were nothing short of miraculous. He was rushed to the General Hospital in St. John's, where a team of dedicated doctors and nurses fought tirelessly to save his life. During those critical first days, Adrian's family faced the constant fear of losing him; medical staff warned repeatedly that his survival was unlikely. His sister Sheila travelled from Port aux Basques, while his mother made frequent trips from Brigus South. His siblings Carmel and Junior, who lived nearby, remained by his side continuously, providing support through this overwhelming ordeal.

As he struggled through the initial stages of recovery, his weakened body became susceptible to further complications—he developed pneumonia, which prolonged his convalescence. He spent about eight months at the St. John's General Hospital before being transferred to the quadriplegic unit of the Queen Mary Veteran's Hospital in Montreal. There, he underwent intensive rehabilitation for another 18 months, working tirelessly to regain any semblance of function and independence.

Upon returning to Newfoundland, Adrian continued his recovery at the Sanitorium on Topsail Road for six months, where he received ongoing physical therapy and support. Eventually, he was moved to the Hoyles Home on Portugal Cove Road, where he would spend the rest of his life, except for the period when he left to attend Dalhousie Law School. He never walked again after the accident. The only movement he had below his neck was in his right hand, and that came after three years of therapy. Although he was unable to grip anything in his right hand, he was able to operate electronic equipment including an electric wheelchair, allowing him a degree of autonomy.

After the accident, Adrian struggled with nightmares, flashbacks, and the weight of adjusting to his new reality. Everyday tasks he once took for granted were now out of reach, and his world felt much smaller. At first, he pulled away from the people around him, unsure of how to accept their help and overwhelmed by the challenges ahead.

Rehabilitation was tough, both on his body and his mind, as he worked to come to terms with the changes in his life. The road wasn't easy, but over time, Adrian started to rely on the support of his friends and family. Their constant love and encouragement gave him the strength to keep going. Slowly, Adrian began to rebuild his life and started to see a future for himself. His story shows how resilience and support can help someone adapt and find hope, even in the toughest time.

After his accident, Adrian's priorities shifted from physical activities to using his mind. As he put it, "After my accident, I couldn't be physically aggressive anymore, so I had to make the most of my mental abilities."

He set his sights on going to university to become a lawyer. It had been 15 years since he finished high school and he knew it wouldn't be easy.

Adrian was accepted to Memorial University of Newfoundland (MUN). In the 1970s, attending classes and moving through campus in a wheelchair required patience and resourcefulness. He persevered and graduated with a bachelor's degree in Arts in 1973 and went on to study law at Dalhousie University in Halifax. After graduation from Dalhousie in 1976, being the first quadriplegic person in North America to do so, he returned to Newfoundland, where he eventually took a position with the Department of Justice.

For the next twenty-five years Adrian worked tirelessly, advocating for the rights and well-being of people with physical disabilities. His relentless efforts led to significant advances in accessibility, inclusivity, and quality of life for individuals with disabilities. Throughout his career, he received numerous national and international awards, which recognized his personal achievements, but also underscored the vital importance of his work in championing an inclusive society.

TWO

The Early Years

TO UNDERSTAND THE MAN ADRIAN BATTCOCK would become, it is important to begin with the place and people who first shaped his life. Adrian Battcock was born in 1935 in the small community of Brigus South, located on Newfoundland's Southern Shore. He was the third child of John (Jack) and Margaret Battcock. Adrian's father, Jack, grew up in this small community where life hadn't changed much from his grandfather's time. From the early part of the nineteenth century up into the middle of the twentieth century, most families in the area made their living through fishing. They also hunted, farmed just enough to get by, and worked in various trades to support themselves. The Battcock family was known for their skills in both carpentry and the fishery, earning them high regard throughout the Southern Shore.

The family also ran a forge, where Jack and his two brothers worked. In the forge they crafted a variety of items including tools, horseshoes, nails, and household items. The local men relied on the blacksmith for repairs to various pieces of fishing equipment and any metal items they used in their daily lives. The forge was also a central area where the local men gathered to discuss community news and share stories. The Battcocks were especially known for their metal work and they were often called upon to create custom items. Some remnants of Jack's work can still be seen in the Cape Broyle graveyard today. Although many of the graves are overgrown with wild plants and berries, hints of his craftsmanship peek through. Adrian was too young to remember his father working in the family forge, but he grew up hearing stories of how fishermen would gather there, and how news seemed to reach the forge before it reached anyone else. In 1931, Jack married Margaret Gregory, also of Brigus South. Like the Battcocks, the Gregorys were a fishing family. At this time, most fishermen used simple, traditional methods, venturing out daily in small boats to earn a living. Their skills and knowledge of the sea were passed down through generations, preserving a rich history of maritime expertise. They had a knack for knowing when to set out and where to find the best catches, but their work wasn't easy. To keep going, they had to respond to whatever the ocean threw at them, relying on their experience and determination to make it through.

Margaret, affectionately known as Maggie, was the eldest of six children with three sisters and two younger brothers. Being the eldest, she took on a significant level of responsibility. This included various household chores as well as helping care for her younger siblings while her parents were busy with other tasks. She also took on a wide range of duties that extended beyond the house, such as tending to gardens and making hay, berry picking, running errands, et cetera.

Maggie's mother, Mary, was a midwife. She was frequently called away from home, leaving Maggie with the duties of the household. Known as "the Doc," Mary Gregory delivered babies and provided general medical care as needed. With the nearest doctor located in St. John's, Mary was called upon at all hours, day or night, to handle various medical situations. In return for her services, she was often compensated with goods like vegetables, meat, or fish. In addition to her work as a midwife and providing general medical assistance, Mary Gregory also cared for those who were dying, offering emotional support to grieving families. She would prepare a recently deceased body for burial and sew the burial attire. She had a particular skill for making shrouds, the garments used to cover the deceased.

In rural Newfoundland, where funeral homes were nonexistent, churches would sometimes serve as the venue for a wake. More commonly, wakes were held in the home of the deceased. Mary Gregory had a special room in her home reserved for such occasions, known as the parlour or front room. Adrian and his siblings remembered this room as being particularly cold and uninviting. At its heart was an organ, which Mary and later her daughter Maggie would play for services and for their personal enjoyment.

Mary was also a milliner, crafting hats for women. The family often joked that she brought people into the world, helped them leave it, and provided a hat for the journey in between. Adrian's memories of his grandmother, Mary, were of an elderly woman who seemed timeless to him—always dressed in long, dark dresses, with her rosary beads never far from her fingers. Maggie inherited a wealth of skills and traditions from Mary, taking on the role of caretaker for the many treasured family heirlooms. Among these were the shrouds, which were tangible links to the past, carrying stories of the generations that came before her. Maggie's children remember using the shrouds for dress-up games.

In 1916, at the age of twenty, Maggie started teaching in the tiny all-grade Catholic school in Brigus South. She continued in this role until her marriage, living at home with her parents and contributing to the family income while assisting her younger siblings. During this period, all-grade schools were common in Newfoundland, especially in small communities and rural areas. Teachers accommodated students of varying ages and abilities within a single classroom. In two-room schools, children often progressed quickly, sometimes completing two years' worth of work in just one year. Teachers maintained close relationships with families in the community and played a significant role in the education and development of children.

Maggie loved her years as a teacher and was well-respected in the community. She believed in the value of education and worked hard to give her students the best start in life. She knew all the children in the community, was familiar with their families, and took a genuine interest in their lives. Her belief in the value of education would go on to influence important decisions she made later in life.

Many of her former students stayed in touch with her over the years, stopping by for a visit or sending her letters letting her know how they were doing. Maggie always enjoyed hearing about their jobs, families, and achievements. Her front room was full of pictures and mementoes of these students. Their visits and letters meant a lot to her, as they were a reminder of the positive difference she had made in their lives.

Throughout the years that Maggie taught school, she also helped out with her younger siblings as they established careers. Her sister, Catherine, became a telegraph officer at the telegraph station at Cape Race, a crucial communication hub. She received and sent messages across the Atlantic. Later on, Catherine left to join the order of Sisters of St. Martha and eventually became a hospital administrator in Glace Bay, Nova Scotia. The two other sisters, Mary and Ella, studied nursing at Glace Bay before returning to Newfoundland to work in various hospitals. Like a lot of other Newfoundlanders at the time, her two brothers, Henry and Mickey, moved to New York in search of better job opportunities. When the last of her siblings left home, Maggie got married.

Jack and Maggie were married in the tiny Catholic Church in Cape Broyle on April 28, 1931, and quickly built a lively, loving household, welcoming four children—Carmel, John (Junior), Adrian, and Sheila—over the next six years. Both in their mid-thirties when they got married, Jack and Maggie had grown up together in the same close-knit community. Their shared expectations for family life created a strong and fulfilling partnership.

Jack had learned carpentry skills from his father, and with the help of his brothers he built a home for his growing family. Jack was employed by the Department of Highways and also managed a forge alongside his brothers. Maggie devoted herself to running the household and raising their children. Maggie had inherited her sewing skills from her mother, and she took great pride in creating clothes for her little ones. She had a particular talent for repurposing old garments, often taking apart an old coat and transforming it into a new outfit for one of the children. Maggie's kindness extended beyond her own family; she generously shared clothing her children had outgrown with neighbours and lent a helping hand whenever it was needed.

The family grew vegetables, raised chickens, kept a cow and a horse. From an early age the children pitched in with chores, helping in the garden, tending to the animals, and assisting with various household tasks.

Maggie's children were close in age, which created a strong bond between them. Despite their chores, they found plenty of time to play outside, no matter the season or weather. They spent hours playing hide-and-seek and tag, darting in and out of the barn and sheds with carefree energy. As soon as the snow melted, they turned to games like hopscotch, marbles, and ball, filling their days with friendly competition. The nearby beaches and woods became their playground, offering endless opportunities for exploration.

During the long winter months, the landscape transformed into a snowy wonderland. The hills, covered in snow, were perfect for sliding, with children racing down the slopes on makeshift slides made from pieces of cardboard or scraps of canvas. When the ponds froze over, they became skating rinks, where the children strapped blades onto their boots and glided across the ice.

During the 1930s most rural and remote communities did not have electricity. Even in areas where electricity was available, its use in households was still somewhat limited. Jack developed a series of small windmills that provided electricity to his home. This allowed the family to have a radio, which was quite a luxury at the time. The children remembered their neighbours dropping into the house to listen to it. Many evenings after supper, the house would come alive with people who gathered to listen to popular radio shows, news updates, and live broadcasts. These were special times. Maggie always had the kettle on, ready to make a cup of tea for everyone. She enjoyed sitting and knitting or sewing, happy to be surrounded by her young children and the lively atmosphere. In those moments, with her home full of people and the comforting buzz of conversation, everything felt just right in the world.

The Catholic Church was central to every aspect of the family's life. It served as a focal point for community gatherings and social events and played a fundamental role in important family ceremonies like baptisms, weddings, and funerals. The Church's teachings on the importance of marriage and parental roles defined their personal philosophies on these matters. Respect for elders, a strong work ethic, and adherence to Catholic teachings were instilled in the children from an early age. The sense of duty to both faith and family shaped their identities, providing a moral framework that guided them throughout their lives.

In 1940, tragedy struck the family when Jack was severely injured in an accident, leaving him bedridden. Maggie did everything she could to care for him, but his health steadily declined. Eventually, he was transferred to a hospital in St. John's, where he passed away on August 27, 1941, at the age of forty-four. Widowed and left to raise her four young children, aged four to eight, Maggie faced an overwhelming loss. While her husband's death left her grieving deeply, and with children too young to fully understand their father's absence, Maggie drew strength from her unwavering faith. Despite moments of sadness, emptiness, and loneliness, her faith became a source of comfort and resilience. Supported by her immediate family and the community, Maggie embraced the difficult job of raising her children alone.

It was also an exceptionally hard time in Newfoundland's history. The early 1930s saw the collapse of the economy. Heavy debts incurred during the construction of the railway, coupled with the financial strain of raising a regiment during World War I, placed an enormous burden on the country. These pressures, compounded by the effects of the Great Depression following the 1929 stock market crash, led to widespread bankruptcy and the eventual collapse of the government. This economic turmoil left the island in a state of severe instability, further adding to the hardship faced by families like Maggie's.

This period of widespread poverty and hardship, during which the collapse of cod prices made it nearly impossible for fishing families to make a living, was the world that Adrian was born into.

When his father died, Adrian was only six years old. Whatever fragile balance the family had managed was suddenly gone. His siblings—Junior, seven; Carmel, eight; and Sheila, four—were also young, leaving Maggie to navigate an incredibly challenging time. Even with support from others, she struggled with limited resources. Seeing her challenges, Maggie's elderly parents asked her to move back in with them for extra help. Her father also reached out to his son Henry in New York, asking him to come home to help his sister Maggie during this difficult period.

THREE

Uncle Henry

HENRY HAD FOLLOWED HIS BROTHER MICKEY to New York in search of work in the early 1930s. Mickey had gone to New York a few years earlier and was now employed by the New York Police Department (NYPD). During this period, there were significant construction projects in New York City, including the building of skyscrapers, bridges, and other infrastructure. Newfoundlanders had a reputation for accepting long hours, knowing that their efforts would be the key to building a stable future for themselves and their families.

Henry was anxious to prove himself and secure a place among the city's industrious workers. While there, Henry often socialized with fellow Newfoundlanders who had also come seeking employment. He was an excellent cook, delighting everyone with hearty, home-style meals that reminded them of the flavours they grew up with. Mickey acted as tour guide and provided a home base for Henry. In the few short years Henry was able to stay in New York, the brothers grew close. From time to time, they would meet up with friends from home and go to parties. At one of these gatherings, Henry met a young woman he hoped to spend more time with—but life had other plans.

When his father sent a telegram requesting his help, Henry didn't hesitate. He immediately arranged passage to Newfoundland, stepping away from his dreams of building a life in New York. Mickey understood better than anyone what Henry was giving up for their sister, while he himself remained in New York with his wife and young family. Before Henry left, Mickey gave him a parting gift—a dark brown oak billy club with ivy inlays, which had kept him safe on the streets of Manhattan. Henry could not have known then that he would never return to New York, and that the brothers would see each other only very infrequently, on the rare occasions when Mickey came home for a visit. As he boarded the ship, Henry couldn't help but wonder what might have been. Over the years, he often thought about that girl, wondering where life had taken her and whether she ever thought of him. Sometimes, in quiet moments, he'd imagine the life they might have shared.

Upon arriving in St. John's, Henry set out on the sixty-mile walk to Brigus South. Along the way, friends and relatives offered him meals and places to rest. As he walked, he reflected on his family's needs, the role he was about to step into, and the values his parents had instilled in him. With each step, he mentally prepared to provide the support Maggie and her children so desperately needed.

Work and opportunity mattered to Henry, but family came first. His actions reflect a sense of duty to family and the belief that when times turn hard, you stand with your own. Henry was a very quiet man, not given to displays of emotion, but his presence carried weight. In the absence of their father, he became a steady, fatherly figure in the children's lives. The children watched him closely and came to respect him deeply.

After returning from New York City, Henry Gregory devoted himself to caring for the family home and providing for his sister and her children. His quiet generosity, unwavering devotion, and selfless commitment earned him the respect and admiration of the entire family.

The Gregory home in Brigus South, Newfoundland.
This is Margaret (Maggie) Gregory Battcock's family home, the house she moved into with her parents when she was widowed.

TOP: Adrian's father's grave in Cape Broyle, Newfoundland. The beautiful iron fence surrounding the family plot was handcrafted by Adrian's father at Battcock Forge. It is a testament to his skill and the pride he took in providing a lasting tribute for his family. It remains a meaningful part of the Battcock family heritage.

RIGHT: Adrian and Junior in the days before Mount Cashel.

FOUR

The School Years: Mount Cashel

MAGGIE WAS DEEPLY CONCERNED ABOUT HER children's well-being. She wrestled with how to meet their basic needs while also ensuring they had opportunities for education and personal growth. Balancing the roles of both parents, Maggie feared falling short in giving her children the direction they required. Seeking counsel, Maggie turned to her parish priest, Father Kennedy, a man she knew well and held in high regard. Father Kennedy an influential figure in the community, recommended that she send her two sons, Adrian and Junior, to St. John's to further their education. In those days, a priest's advice was seldom questioned.

In Newfoundland at the time, families often sent their children to an orphanage if one parent had passed away. The belief was rooted in practicality rather than a lack of love. Orphanages were seen as institutions that could provide a structured environment, better access to education, and basic needs that a struggling parent or extended family might not be able to offer. However, the emotional impact was often profound for the children involved.

Parents or guardians made these choices under immense pressure, believing they were acting in the best interest of the children. Nevertheless, the decision was rarely made without significant anguish, and the same was true in Maggie's case.

Although she was reluctant to send her young boys—aged seven and eight—away, especially to an orphanage, Maggie understood the importance of securing a good education for them. Putting her own feelings aside, she made the heart-wrenching decision to send Adrian and Junior to Mount Cashel Orphanage in St. John's, hoping that this would offer them a better future. Father Kennedy made arrangements for Adrian and Junior to enroll by the end of the summer, just in time for the start of the school year, marking the beginning of a new chapter in their lives.

Mount Cashel Orphanage was built in 1898 by the Roman Catholic archdiocese of St. John's. Bishop Howley donated land from his family's estate for the structure. It was named after the Rock of Cashel in Tipperary, Ireland, from where many of the Irish who settled in Newfoundland had originated. The orphanage was run by the Irish Christian Brothers, a lay order of Catholic men who came to Newfoundland in the latter part of the nineteenth century. It was a huge facility situated on a sizable piece of land on the outskirts of St. John's.

The orphanage provided basic necessities such as food, clothing, and shelter, as well as education and vocational training to prepare the boys for adulthood. The orphanage was run by the Catholic Church but was also supported by donations from individuals, the congregations and parishes as well as from private business enterprises. It was also partially sustained by farmland that was cultivated to provide a supply of vegetables and dairy products. The children at the orphanage helped tend to the crops and animals, learning valuable skills while contributing to their own sustenance.

It is now known that serious abuse took place at Mount Cashel in later years, causing lasting harm to many boys. This painful reality casts a long shadow, though it was completely unknown to families like Maggie's at the time.

When the day arrived for Adrian and Junior to leave, Maggie arranged for Uncle Aubrey Battcock to drive them to St. John's, where he lived. Aubrey was a cousin of Maggie's late husband and was a steady and loyal supporter of the family. What could have been a long and frightening trip for Junior and Adrian was made easier by Aubrey's thoughtfulness. He brought small treats for the journey—fresh apples and soft drinks. Even more important were Aubrey's promises of Christmas visits —promises he never failed to keep.

Aubrey remained a constant presence in the Battcock family's lives. He visited often and took a genuine interest in each of the children as they grew. In time, he earned the affectionate nickname "the family's Patron Saint of Good Deeds." He made sure the boys arrived safely in St. John's. His steady presence reassured the boys that they were not completely alone in this new and uncertain chapter, and it eased some of Maggie's worries as well.

Maggie had carefully prepared for their departure, packing clothing and other essentials. She pinned a Miraculous Medal to several pieces of clothing and packed a holy picture for each of them to keep by their bedside. She travelled with them to the orphanage, doing her best to hide any worry or sadness so they would feel supported and safe in their new surroundings. Junior was just a year older than Adrian but he was a more serious child and took on the role of looking out for his brother.

Maggie never shared her thoughts or emotions as she walked away from the orphanage that day. With quiet strength, she put her own pain aside. Maggie demonstrated a profound selflessness, driven by the hope that this difficult choice would give Adrian and Junior opportunities she couldn't provide on her own. Her love for them was unwavering, even in the face of such a profound separation. Leaving her boys at the orphanage was the hardest decision Maggie ever had to make. The day itself matched her mood—it was a gloomy, overcast day in September. As she walked away from them, her heart felt so heavy it was as if her feet could barely move. Every step was an effort, weighed down by the ache of leaving her sons behind. But Maggie knew she couldn't let them see her hesitate. She straightened her shoulders, forcing herself to walk steadily, holding back the tears and keeping her head high until she was out of their sight.

On the lonely trip back to Brigus South, Maggie could think of nothing else. The silence around her felt overwhelming, and every mile away from the orphanage made her heart ache more. She replayed the scene in her mind, seeing their small faces watching her go, wondering if they understood why she had to leave them. Doubt crept in with every turn of the road. Had she made the right decision? Would they be alright without her? The familiar landscape outside her window felt strangely empty as she wrestled with the guilt and sorrow of parting from her boys. By the time she reached home, she felt exhausted, drained from both the journey and the heartache that filled it.

The house felt empty without her boys, every corner echoing with their absence. Maggie tried to keep herself busy, forcing herself to do chores so she wouldn't dwell on thoughts of them. But as evening fell, the quietness around her grew deeper, making it harder to push away the memories. She lay in bed, unable to sleep, her mind filled with images of her sons. When she finally drifted off, she dreamt that they came rushing into the kitchen, laughing and asking for a slice of bread and jam, just like they used to.

In their hurry, they left the door wide open to the yard. She was always reminding them to close the door. Startled awake, Maggie lay there for a moment, realizing it was only a dream. She went downstairs, hoping somehow they'd be there. The door, of course, was shut tight. The sight brought a lump to her throat, and she wished more than anything that she could turn back time, to a day when her biggest worry was reminding them to close the door behind them. Now, she would have given anything to have them back, even if just to gently scold them once more.

Many years later, Adrian described arriving at Mount Cashel to his niece, Jeanine.

> I remember sitting next to my mother that day in the car. I sat as close to her as I could get. I felt cold and lonely and didn't understand why I couldn't be like all the other children who went to the local school and went home at night—but they had fathers and that made all the difference. We entered the grounds and I remember passing the two stone pillars and seeing the enormous building ahead. It was only then, seeing it up close, that it finally sank in: we weren't just visiting; we were here to stay. When it was time to say goodbye to our mother I couldn't stop crying. But she was as brave as always saying that before we knew it Christmas would be here and we would go to Uncle Aubrey's for our holidays. Every time I went through the gates after that day, I remembered that sad goodbye.

The orphanage was loud and busy, and at first, Adrian and Junior found it a bit overwhelming. They looked around nervously, taking in all the new faces and strange surroundings. It was hard to accept that they were on their own, but they were glad to have each other. Adrian and Junior explored the orphanage side by side, staying close as they got used to their new home. As they wandered through the hallways and around the corners, their bond grew tighter. They felt a little braver knowing they didn't have to face it all alone.

> Junior and I were so intimidated when we entered the halls of Mount Cashel. We held hands and walked into the Brother Superior's office. I remember the smell of the varnish and how the walls glistened in the sun. There were statues and religious paintings everywhere. I joked to Junior that it seemed we were at a church camp. Everything seemed so big—the hallways and the rooms were enormous and the ceilings were so high. There were silver pipes running along every wall and every now and again, they would give off a hissing sound. I felt a spark of rebellion at that moment. Junior warned me to keep quiet—he could sense the nervous energy coming from me. He was now the *man of the family*, and he thought often of the promise he had made to our mother to look after me. He kept that promise for the rest of his life.

They quickly adjusted to the daily routine of the orphanage, finding some comfort in its structure and predictability. Adrian vividly recalled:

> Each morning, we woke to the ringing of a bell, the signal that the day had begun. We slept in a large dormitory shared with forty other boys, and the hum of activity began almost immediately. After washing and dressing, we lined up in single file and made our way to St. Raphael's Chapel for morning Mass.
>
> Breakfast followed in the dining hall, which felt huge to me—the largest room I'd ever been in. The long tables and

> benches stretched forever, with a serving table positioned prominently in the center. Before the meal, we said Grace together, and then sat down to eat. Breakfast was simple and never changed: porridge and toast. The porridge was often cold and lumpy, and the toast slightly burned, but no matter what was on the plate, I ate it without complaint. Once breakfast was finished, the day's chores and activities began. The boys dispersed into their assigned groups. I made sure to stay close to Junior; he seemed to know exactly what to do, and I trusted him to show me the ropes.

Life at the orphanage was structured out of necessity. With so many boys and only a handful of caregivers, everything had to follow a strict schedule. Over time, the boys got used to the routines and began to see the opportunities the place offered. They also formed strong friendships with each other, which helped make the new environment feel a bit more like home. Despite all of this, Adrian found himself struggling to adjust to life in the orphanage. He was overwhelmed by a profound sense of loss, an ache that seemed to deepen with each passing day. The absence of his mother weighed heavily on him, and even though Junior stood by him, Adrian found it impossible to hide the longing for home and family. Beneath that longing was the unresolved grief of his father's death, a loss that had already fractured his sense of safety and belonging. Now, with his mother gone too, the pain of losing his father came rushing back and felt even harder to bear. In those early days he made multiple attempts to escape the orphanage, determined to find his way back home. But after each failed attempt, he began to realize that no matter how far he ran, he couldn't bring back what he'd lost or make things the way they once were.

Adrian threw himself into his studies and extracurricular activities and in no time, his hard work paid off and he excelled in academics and sports. He became quite the athlete. He was tall and well built and became a formidable opponent in both hockey and baseball. At Mount Cashel, sports were an important part of daily life, keeping the boys busy and teaching them valuable lessons. The belief was that team sports helped build discipline, teamwork, and a sense of accomplishment. Engaging in physical activities also provided a way to burn off energy, cope with stress, and make friends while learning skills like cooperation and perseverance.

Mount Cashel teams took part in every sports competition in the city and excelled in each one. The sports activities were integrated into both the overall curriculum and the recreational program. On weekends, the Christian Brothers would take the boys outside the city, encouraging them to run, climb trees, wrestle, and build their strength, turning them into tough athletes. Adrian's name became synonymous with the Mount Cashel teams. He was a steady presence on the hockey team, known more for his grit and reliability than any flashy moves on the ice. His teammates appreciated that he could be counted on to do the little things right—sticking to his position, making solid passes, and keeping the energy up through every game.

Mount Cashel's indoor swimming pool, one of the few in the city, often drew children from outside the orphanage. These visits allowed the boys to make new friends, share laughter, and take part in friendly competitions. For the boys, it was a rare opportunity to connect with the outside world and escape their usual routines. Swimming together was a chance to simply be kids.

Mount Cashel also had a well-known music program, with several bands and choirs. Students were encouraged to participate, as music was seen as an important part of their education. Adrian and Junior both auditioned for the choir; however, their singing abilities were deemed inadequate. They were placed at the back of the choir, instructed to "mouth the words" rather than sing out loud. This was especially hard for Adrian, who loved singing and had a great sense of rhythm. Even though he spoke up about it, the decision to keep him in the background didn't change. It was a tough experience for him and left a lasting impact. His desire to sing freely never went away.

Soon after Adrian and Junior arrived at Mount Cashel, they became friends with another student, Robert (Bob) McGrath. They shared classes and took part in many of the same activities. Bob, with his beautiful tenor voice, was always placed in the front row of the choir and frequently selected for solo performances. Adrian and Junior were genuinely pleased that Bob was chosen for the solo performances, though they couldn't help wishing that one day one of them might be chosen too. Eventually, Adrian and Junior would come to realize there would be other opportunities for singing. In the Battcock family, there was a lighthearted saying: "God gave us the will to sing, but not the voice to match," a playful reminder of their love for music, even if they weren't choir material. They sang anyway, whether they were in key or not, because for them the joy was in the singing, not the sound.

Meals at the orphanage were meagre, mostly consisting of simple staples like porridge, plain bread, and soups or stews with just a few vegetables. The portions were small, barely enough to feed growing children, let alone satisfy their hunger. Adrian often found himself hungry, longing for the hearty meals he enjoyed when he visited home. During mealtime, he would sit next to his friend Bob McGrath. Knowing Adrian's constant hunger, Bob would cover his plate with his arm to keep Adrian from stealing his food. He'd say, "You've got your own plate, Adrian—stick to it!" Adrian would laugh and wait for another opportunity to grab something from Bob's plate.

Many nights, Adrian and a few other boys schemed to sneak into the food storage areas, partly because they were hungry and partly for the excitement and fun of it. They waited until the night watchman finished his rounds, then moved swiftly and quietly. They whispered to each other as they crept through the halls, fully aware of the risk. The fear of getting caught and punished lingered, but their hunger always pushed them to take the chance.

On one of these escapades, Adrian managed to get himself stuck in the dumbwaiter. Long after the incident, the story of his misadventure became a favourite among friends and family. Each time it was retold, it grew more colourful, with new embellishments and exaggerations. Right from the start, it was clear that Adrian had a special gift for storytelling. He also developed a lifelong passion for food, seeing it as more than just a necessity—it was also a way to bring people together and celebrate.

On another occasion, Adrian decided he'd had enough of class and figured he'd pretend to be sick to get a day off. He put on his best pitiful face and convinced everyone he was too unwell to leave his bed. It was all going perfectly—until around lunchtime when the smell of stew from the kitchen drifted upstairs. The smell was too tempting, and he couldn't help himself. Adrian snuck down to the kitchen for a bowl, forgetting all about his sickness in his rush to eat. Of course, he got caught, stew spoon in hand. Adrian was always up to mischief. Years later, Junior would remark, "I slept every night with one eye open, never knowing what he was up to!"

October 24 marked the feast day of St. Raphael, the patron of the chapel at Mount Cashel. On this day, the boys were treated to a special meal in celebration. The highlight was an egg—a simple yet rare treat for many of them. For some, it was their first time tasting an egg, and they savoured it slowly, appreciating its unique flavour. However, a few of the boys, unaccustomed to the richness, found their stomachs unsettled after eating it. For Adrian and Junior, eggs weren't anything special since their family raised hens. During the summer, they'd have one every morning for breakfast. Adrian couldn't resist teasing the other boys at Mount Cashel. He'd say things like, "What's the big deal? I've been eating eggs for so long I'll soon be able to lay one."

Another favourite meal was on Pancake Day, celebrated on Shrove Tuesday, the day before Ash Wednesday and 46 days before Easter Sunday. Pancakes were served for supper rather than breakfast and were often topped with molasses or jam. In many Newfoundland homes, small coins, buttons, or rings were added to the batter, turning the meal into a lighthearted tradition on the eve of Lent. At Mount Cashel, the boys were also served pancakes for supper, but without the treats or sweet toppings. There was no jam topping and no hidden treasures in the batter—only a small dollop of margarine on each plate. Even so, they looked forward to it.

Sometimes, the boys got a chance to head into the city. Once a month, they were given fifteen cents to visit the Nickel Theatre, a small cinema run by the Christian Brothers. They didn't need to pay for admission because their numbered socks, part of the orphanage's laundry system, showed they were from Mount Cashel. This little perk made them feel special, even if only for a short while. With their fifteen cents, they would buy a snack—usually some popcorn or candy—to enjoy during the movie. Sitting in the theatre, they felt a rare sense of escape, getting lost in the stories on the screen. After the movie, they often lingered outside, not wanting the freedom to end. Sometimes, they'd wander downtown to meet friends, stretching their time away as long as they could. On occasion, they would miss their ride back to the orphanage, which always meant trouble. They felt it was worth it.

Across the road from Mount Cashel was a small corner store where children from the nearby schools would hang out in the afternoons. The boys weren't supposed to leave the orphanage grounds, but Adrian usually found a way to sneak across the road. Whenever he had some money, he'd buy a Pepsi and an apricot square and eat it as fast as he could, enjoying every last bite. He'd stick around the shop, joking with the local girls just to make them giggle.

There was one girl, in particular, who caught Adrian's eye. She had a quick smile and a spark in her eyes, and she seemed to enjoy his jokes more than the others. Sometimes, she'd give him a playful nudge or laugh a little louder than the rest. Adrian couldn't quite figure her out, but he kept finding excuses to hang around the shop. Because he was growing up in the orphanage, his chances to be around girls were few and far between. He soon learned, however, that a bit of charm, a ready smile, and a well-timed joke could go a long way in catching a girl's attention. It was during one of these outings that he picked up smoking. He got his first cigarette from an older boy, and though he coughed his way through it, he was hooked almost immediately. He loved everything about it—the way the smoke curled, the sense of rebellion, and the camaraderie it brought. When he couldn't afford pre-rolled cigarettes, he'd scrounge up loose tobacco and papers, becoming surprisingly resourceful. Before long, he earned a reputation at the orphanage as the go-to guy for smokes. He even became something of a mentor, teaching the other boys how to blow smoke rings and sharing tips for masking the telltale smell of tobacco. Despite his best efforts to stay under the radar, he was caught one night puffing by an open window. He'd convinced himself the smoke would drift outside, but instead, it gave him away. His biggest concern wasn't the punishment—it was the thought of them telling his mother during her next visit. The idea of her disappointment was worse than anything the orphanage staff could dish out.

Twice a year, in the fall and spring, Maggie came to St. John's to visit her boys. In the days leading up to her visits, she busied herself preparing gifts from home, knitting them new socks to keep their feet warm and baking their favourite treats. She knew how much these small comforts from home meant to them, so she filled tins with cookies, fresh bread, and jars of her homemade jams. She stayed with relatives during her visits to St. John's and walked the hour-long trip to the orphanage each day. Maggie talked with the boys about what they were doing, how they were adjusting, and any struggles they were facing. She also made a point of meeting with the staff, learning how Adrian and Junior were adapting and addressing any issues they faced. Maggie made sure that everyone knew her boys had family looking out for them, advocating for their needs, and ensuring their progress was never overlooked.

Adrian worried that his mother would be told about some of the mischief he'd been up to and after each visit, he'd say to Junior: "I dodged a bullet this time." Years later, long after Adrian had left the orphanage, he asked his mother if she'd ever heard about the trouble he'd gotten into. She admitted, "Yes, I did." Surprised, he said, "You never mentioned it to me." She smiled and replied, "No, because when I saw your little face looking up at me, wondering if I was going to say anything, I thought, *I can't upset him and then have to leave, so I'll say nothing*. I knew you would be okay and I trusted Junior would look after you."

Every visit brought Maggie closer to her sons, who always looked forward to her arrival. She'd remind them to say their prayers and treat others with kindness and respect. Her love and guidance were a constant in their lives, and her visits gave them strength and reassurance. Each time Maggie had to leave, a heavy tug of worry stayed with her until her next visit. She hugged them tightly, savouring the moments before saying goodbye, always reminding them to look out for each other and be good. As the years passed, Adrian's bond with his mother only grew stronger.

After Jack passed away, Maggie moved back to her parents' house in Brigus South, bringing her two young daughters with her. Living with her parents was tough but offered the support she needed during a difficult time. Mary's parlour was still occasionally used for wakes. Shortly after moving back to the ancestral home, Sheila recalls running into the kitchen one morning and saying to her mother "There's a woman asleep in the parlour." Unbeknownst to her, the previous evening, after the children had gone to bed, a body had been quietly brought into the house for a wake.

One of Maggie's greatest joys was spending Sunday evenings playing the organ. After a long and busy week, these moments of music and reflection offered her a sense of solace and renewal. Yet, even as the melodies filled the room, a deep sadness often shadowed her expression. Perhaps she was remembering happier days or thinking of the weight of the burdens she carried. Her heart was heavy with constant worry about her boys, and she often questioned her decision to place them in the orphanage, a choice that lingered with painful doubt. Sunday evenings were particularly hard, as the quiet allowed her fears about their future to surface. Tears would slip down her cheeks as she grappled with whether she had done the right thing in sending her sons to Mount Cashel. Though the music brought her brief comfort, it was often replaced by sorrow, a poignant reminder of another week passing without her boys at home.

Within a few years of Maggie moving home, her parents passed away. Her two sisters, Mary and Ella, both nurses, came home to help her care for their parents during their final days. Having her sisters around made things a bit easier for Maggie, bringing some moments of laughter as they united to care for each other. After her parents passed away, Maggie found some comfort in maintaining the family home, holding onto the traditions and values that had always been important to them. Later, Maggie provided the same care and attention to her in-laws in their last moments. In time, she settled into a quieter routine with her two girls and Henry, finding comfort in the day-to-day routines.

FIVE

Visits Home

EVERY JUNE, ADRIAN AND JUNIOR WOULD GO home to Brigus South for the summer months. The boys couldn't wait to be with their family. Their two sisters, Carmel and Sheila, would plan fun things for them to do together. Summers seemed to last forever, and years later, the boys recalled the days always being bright and sunny. Sheila fondly remembers the long walks she and Adrian would take to Cape Broyle to visit Coady's store to buy candy. They took their time walking home, stopping to pick up smooth rocks or leaves or bird's nests or insects along the way. Sometimes, they would catch a butterfly or poke at an ant hill watching the ants scurrying around. They'd be gone for hours without anyone noticing they'd left.

The summers allowed Adrian and Junior to settle back into family life and provided a reprieve from the structured environment of the orphanage. They spent a lot of time outdoors playing with friends and enjoying themselves—the long summer days were filled with picking berries, helping Uncle Henry with the hay, feeding the cows, and swimming in the ponds around Brigus South.

Maggie had resumed working after her husband's death. Her sister Catherine had worked at the Cape Race telegraph station and taught Maggie all she knew about Morse Code. Maggie caught on very quickly and before long, she found herself quite proficient, able to send and receive messages with confidence. Maggie took on the role of a telegraph officer, working from her own home. With the office set up in the house, Maggie's children found themselves immersed in the world of telegraphy. They'd be called upon to deliver messages around the community, a task that made them familiar with every house and its occupants.

The boys also got up to mischief. One day, Junior and Adrian decided to buy a bottle of moonshine from the local bootlegger. Junior was chosen to go inside while Adrian stood watch. After a few minutes, Junior emerged empty-handed. Determined, Adrian decided to give it a try. To Junior's amazement, Adrian came out shortly afterward carrying a bottle of moonshine. He grinned mysteriously, keeping the secret of how he'd charmed the shopkeeper. Their next challenge was to ensure their mother didn't discover the illicit bottle. They cleverly hid it in the barn, out of sight. Later that evening, under the cover of darkness, they snuck out to the barn with a few close friends. Sitting in a circle, they passed the bottle around; the taste was harsh, but the sense of rebellion and adventure made it worthwhile.

Maggie was always worried about the boys and did everything she could to keep them out of trouble and on the right track. When they came home for the summers, they were a novelty in the community; their time in the city made them stand out, and everyone wanted to be around them. Maggie kept a close eye on where they went and who they spent time with, especially since she knew the influence of others could lead them astray. To steer them away from certain people or activities, she often got creative. In one instance, she warned them that particular girls had nits to keep them from getting too close. Maggie's imagination knew no limits—she could come up with the most elaborate stories to keep her boys safe and on the path she envisioned for them.

Maggie worked tirelessly all year long, with summers being especially busy. During the warm months, she would pick berries to turn into homemade jam. The children eagerly accompanied her on these outings, loving every moment of it. They spent hours picking berries, often eating as many as they collected. They would bring along a picnic and find a comfortable spot to enjoy it—somehow, the sandwiches always tasted better outdoors than they ever did at home. The hills around Brigus South were rich with raspberries, blueberries, bakeapples, and partridgeberries, each providing a different flavour for the jams. She picked enough berries to ensure there would be plenty of jam to last through the long winter months and she always had a bottle to share.

In the fall, Maggie would turn her attention to making pickles, using the rhubarb, onions, and other vegetables from their garden. She took great care in preparing the ingredients, combining them with spices and vinegar to create jars of tangy, flavourful pickles. These pickles were a staple in the family's meals during the colder months. Maggie's kitchen would be filled with the savoury aroma of the pickling process, a scent that signalled the changing of the seasons and the care she put into providing for her family year round.

Uncle Henry was a role model to the boys. Upon returning from New York, he had resumed his fishing routine, drawing on the skills he'd learned while working with his father before his trip. It was as if he had never left, effortlessly picking up where he had left off. In the early years, he fished alone in a small open boat. Rising as early as 3 a.m., he would push off from the wharf in his small open boat, bait his hand lines, and head out alone to set and haul his gear in the quiet dawn. By 8 a.m., he would be back home. It was very hard work but he enjoyed it. There was always something to do—mending fishing gear, making sure the sheds and stores were in order, and doing work on the wharf. Another role Henry took on was that of community barber. He set up a chair in his shed on the wharf, positioning it near a window to make the most of the natural light. A mirror was propped against the wall, and his simple tools—a comb, scissors, and straight razor—rested on a small table close at hand. Neighbours would drop in for a trim and often stayed longer than they intended. He charged just ten cents for a haircut, and if someone couldn't pay, Henry never made mention of it. Junior and Adrian helped by spreading the fish on flakes or rocks to dry, and cutting out cod tongues. Sometimes, they sold the tongues, earning a little pocket money and feeling proud of their hard work. They loved sitting on the wharf listening to the older men telling stories. Adrian later remembered those times as important, where he not only developed a love for storytelling but also felt a strong bond with the history and toughness of the community. He'd recall how the tales shared by the older men shaped his view of life and gave him a deeper understanding of where he came from.

The family also set out gardens with potatoes, carrots, turnip, cabbage, and beet. They kept cows, sheep, and chickens. One of the children's favourite chores was spreading caplin over the gardens. These tiny fish would come ashore in early summer to spawn, drawing crowds to the beaches and creating a flurry of activity in the community. The children would rush to the shore with buckets and nets, excitedly collecting the fish to use as fertilizer for the gardens, turning this chore into a fun tradition. Maggie would prepare a meal of fresh caplin, while Henry salted and smoked some to enjoy later.

The house was heated by a woodstove, making a steady supply of firewood essential during the harsh winters. In the kitchen, one of the boards directly above the stove was missing—a common feature in Newfoundland homes at the time, allowing heat to rise to the rooms upstairs. The children would gather around that opening, listening in on the conversations below. Adrian later recalled that he learned countless things this way, absorbing stories and lessons even if, at the time, he didn't always understand their full meaning.

Henry would cut wood and haul it home with the help of his loyal horse, Nell. More than just a reliable worker, Nell was a beloved family pet, known for her dependable nature. The children adored her, often sneaking her treats and enjoying her gentle companionship. They would take her for walks, letting her lead the way while they chatted and laughed. Every Sunday morning, Henry could be seen riding in the dray with Nell as they made the journey to Cape Broyle for Mass. During this time, Newfoundland ponies roamed freely across the land, and there were a good number of them in Brigus South. Small but sturdy, they wandered along the lanes and grazed in open meadows. Though they seemed almost wild, many belonged to local families and were used for hauling firewood or ploughing the gardens. Children would stop to pet them or feed them crab apples or cabbage leaves. They mixed in with the goats that also roamed freely. The goats were blamed for eating anything in sight including lost mittens and hats. On Sundays, Maggie liked to cook a chicken for dinner—one of the chickens they raised would have to be killed for the meal. This usually fell to Junior and Adrian. Junior hated the task of killing the chicken, while Adrian, with an impish streak, was amused by the sight of the chicken running around without its head. Back at the orphanage, Adrian would eagerly recount to the other boys how the headless chickens ran around, usually embellishing the story with exaggerated details about how long it continued to move and what it looked like while doing so.

On many Sundays, after Mass, the priest would drop in for a cup of tea. Maggie laid out a spread of baked goods with jams and pickles, creating a warm and welcoming atmosphere. The children knew what was expected of them on these visits and sat quietly, speaking politely when addressed. However, not all encounters with the priest were pleasant. One time, the priest asked Henry to drive him to Tors Cove to visit some parishioners. Henry was happy to help and agreed right away—but he was observant and not one to miss what was going on around him. When they got there, the priest went into the house, leaving Henry and Nell waiting outside in the cold. What was supposed to be a quick visit ended up lasting two hours, much longer than Henry had expected. Nobody questioned the priest's actions, as his authority in such things was simply taken for granted. Henry never forgot it.

Being self-sufficient and hard-working wasn't just important, it was necessary for survival in Newfoundland at the time. During the summers, Junior and Adrian helped out wherever they could, driven by their admiration for their Uncle Henry. With Henry's patient guidance, they learned practical skills that would serve them well later in life. Henry kept himself busy; he painted the house every year, whether it needed it or not. The colours were never planned. He simply gathered the small amounts of leftover paint sitting in tins in the shed and mixed them together, and whatever shade emerged became that year's colour. On one occasion, he combined the bright orange from the house trim with the black used on the shed floorboards, and the inside stairs turned a rich, deep mahogany. No one could ever have duplicated his exact blends, but more often than not, the results turned out surprisingly well.

Henry liked to hunt birds and would head out turr (a type of seabird) hunting each fall with his 12-gauge shotgun. He was careful to keep his gun clean and safely stored when not in use. Setting off in his open boat as the weather turned crisp, he followed a ritual he had practised for years. He had a great knack for plucking the feathers and cleaning the birds, and he would hang them in his shed, where the cold air preserved them until they were ready to be cooked. He was known for making a delicious, hearty stew that rarely lasted long once it was set on the table. Henry was also a jack of all trades; he could turn his hand to almost anything. He once came into possession of an old, discarded clock. Somehow, he managed to make it work by placing a razor blade inside it. That clock lasted for the rest of Henry's life, and it is now owned by his nephew—still working to this day.

Both Adrian and Junior had birthdays in the summer, and their family always made sure to recognize the special days. Even though there wasn't any money for gifts or parties, their mother and sisters would find ways to mark the occasions. On one birthday, Maggie baked a cake and planned a small picnic in the backyard. The sandwiches and juice were arranged on the table alongside the cake. But in the twinkling of an eye, Nell, their faithful horse, nudged her way in and took a big bite out of the cake. Maggie just shook her head and sighed, "Well, I suppose she needed a treat too."

SIX

Returning to Mount Cashel

THE SUMMERS FLEW BY QUICKLY AND BEFORE they knew it, Adrian and Junior were saying goodbye to the carefree days and returning to the routine of school life in St. John's. Mount Cashel organized various fundraisers throughout the year, with the most popular being the annual Christmas Raffle. It was held in a storefront on Water Street for two or three weeks, right in the heart of the bustling Christmas shopping season. Water Street buzzed with holiday activity, and the raffle became a central attraction. It involved the sale of tickets offering the chance to win an array of prizes donated by local businesses and supporters. The raffle prizes often included live fowl, such as chickens, turkeys, and ducks, which were kept in the storefront alongside displays of various cuts of meat. The atmosphere was lively, with shoppers darting in and out of the building as prizes were awarded every hour.

The boys from the orphanage played an active role in selling tickets, going door-to-door in neighbourhoods or setting up booths ahead of the event. One of the favourite jobs during the raffle was working the microphone. This involved announcing the event to people passing by and encouraging them to come in and buy tickets. It was a popular role among the boys because it let them interact with the community and play an important part in making the fundraiser a success. Bob McGrath, chosen for his clear and pleasant speaking voice, was excited to take on the job. He enjoyed the experience, and his natural talent made him the envy of the other boys. Bob stayed close friends with both Junior and Adrian. They spent a lot of time together and years later, Bob became their brother-in-law when he married their sister Sheila.

Since there wasn't any money for the boys to travel home for Christmas, they stayed in St. John's with family. Uncle Aubrey made Christmas magical for Adrian and Junior. As soon as their last class before the break ended, they would rush to the windows, eagerly waiting to be picked up. The night before, they could hardly sleep, too excited about spending the next two weeks away from the orphanage with family. The holidays felt like a real break, full of laughter. On Christmas Eve, the adults would put handmade decorations on the tree and everyone would bundle up in warm coats and scarves and go off to the Basilica for midnight Mass. Upon waking on Christmas morning, they would find a stocking filled with an array of treats—occasionally an orange and an apple, perhaps a new pair of mitts. The sight of an orange was a rare delight, reserved solely for Christmas.

During the winter break, they would walk down to Water Street to look at displays in the shop windows, or go skating on the frozen ponds around the city. Back at the house, they'd spend hours playing in the snow, having snowball fights or setting up a game of hockey with whatever they could find for sticks and a puck. The holidays would go on until Old Christmas Day on January 6, when everyone would gather once again for a final meal before the boys returned to the orphanage. Years later, Adrian and Junior spoke fondly of those unforgettable Christmases, which highlighted the importance of family and community in shaping their lives.

During their time at the orphanage, one school year rolled into the next, and the routine brought a certain stability to their lives, even as the years seemed to stretch endlessly. Before they knew it, ten years had passed. Along the way, they forged friendships that were as close as family, strengthened by shared games, whispered secrets, and the comfort of leaning on one another through small triumphs and disappointments. Time was often measured by the weeks until summer or the start of a new school year, each marking a step in a childhood shaped by both joy and hardship.

Adrian and Junior stayed at Mount Cashel from 1942 to 1952. These formative years left an indelible mark on their lives, shaping their character and future paths. Junior's children fondly remember when they visited St. John's, their father would drive them up to Mount Cashel, pointing out the exact locations of his and Adrian's room, sharing vivid details about their experiences there. He held Mount Cashel in such high regard, attributing its influence to shaping his life in positive ways.

Adrian had many fond memories of Mount Cashel as well. Although there were times when he felt lonely and missed his family, the years there taught him to be independent and resourceful. Even in the quiet or difficult moments, those experiences shaped him and stayed with him long after he left. Adrian was a very pragmatic person. He often said, "Mount Cashel was a good place to grow up. I made friends, learned a lot, and we always looked out for each other. Sure, it wasn't home, but I wouldn't trade those years for anything."

SEVEN

Life After Mount Cashel

LIKE MOST BOYS WHO GREW UP IN THE ORPHANAGE, Adrian moved on after completing high school. Several families in St. John's welcomed the boys from Mount Cashel as boarders. Adrian and Junior were placed in different homes; Junior and Bob McGrath were taken in by the Walsh family on Hamilton Avenue, while Adrian stayed with the Murphy family on Bond Street. This marked the first time the brothers were separated, setting them on different paths that would shape their futures in distinct ways.

Living in different homes meant getting used to new families and routines, but the boys stayed close, visiting each other often to catch up. Adrian shared a bedroom with the Murphy boys and felt like he truly belonged in their family. He enjoyed the hearty meals and raved about the friendly and lively neighbourhood. Junior's experience with the Walsh family was just as positive. Both he and Adrian settled into their new homes, found jobs, and started getting on with their lives.

When Junior got his first paycheck, he bought a new coat and loaned it to Adrian. A few days later, when Junior asked for it back

Adrian shrugged and said, "I gave it to a homeless man I met on the street. He could've been one of us from Mount Cashel. I thought he needed it more than I did, so I gave him the coat and a little money." Junior pretended to be upset at first, but he was actually deeply moved by his brother's compassion.

On Sundays, Adrian would head over to Hamilton Avenue to pick up Junior, and together they'd walk to visit their sister Sheila at Littledale College on Waterford Bridge Road. The brothers, tall and good-looking, turned heads as they walked through the streets. Sheila, with her own striking looks and graceful presence, added to the impression the trio made. Their strong family resemblance and charm stood out, and it didn't take long for the girls at Littledale to take notice. Years later, when Sheila had a baby, she was delighted by how many of her friends offered to babysit. It wasn't until later that she realized it wasn't the baby they were interested in—it was her brothers.

By the time Adrian left Mount Cashel in 1952, St. John's was a busy city. Much of its energy coming from the nearby American military base, Fort Pepperrell, at Pleasantville which had been established during World War II. The base brought considerable economic activity and a sense of modernity to the area. American soldiers and their families contributed to the local economy by frequenting shops, bars, and restaurants, and their presence had a noticeable cultural impact on the city. The base itself was a small, self-contained community with its own amenities, including housing, schools, recreational facilities, and even a theatre. This influx of American culture introduced new fashions, music, and consumer goods to the city, creating a dynamic blend of traditional Newfoundland life and contemporary influences from the United States.

Adrian found himself in the thick of things while working at the American base at Fort Pepperrell. Living downtown, he was well placed to witness the social dynamics that played out between the local boys and the American servicemen. The base was a hub of activity, and the influx of Americans brought a certain excitement to the social scene in St. John's. Local boys often found themselves in competition with the American soldiers for the attention of the local girls. The Americans, with their modern clothes, foreign accents, and access to luxury goods, had an exotic allure that made them attractive to many.

However, Adrian stood out in this competition. He had a magnetic personality and a charm that set him apart from both his peers and the American newcomers. He attracted people because of who he was—optimistic and full of life. While many boys tried to win attention by mimicking the Americans or showcasing their own local bravado, Adrian's authenticity shone through. His ability to navigate both worlds—local and American—gave him a unique edge in this spirited, sometimes tense social landscape.

Approximately 40,000 Newfoundland women married American servicemen during the decades-long presence of United States military bases in the region, including Fort Pepperrell and other installations at Argentia and Stephenville. This phenomenon was sometimes referred to as the "friendly invasion." Some of these brides ended up in places like New York, Boston, and beyond. For many young women, marrying an American represented both adventure and opportunity—an escape from the familiar routines of island life into the promise of something bigger.

A popular gathering place for young people during this time was the Blue Puttee on Rawlins Cross. The Blue Puttee was a lively social hub where locals and Americans mingled, danced, and enjoyed the vibrant post-war nightlife. The friendly competition between Newfoundland boys and the well-dressed American soldiers played out in venues like this, adding an element of intrigue and rivalry to the city's evolving social dynamics. Adrian quickly became known for his ability to catch the attention of the girls.

It was during this time that Screech earned its name. The tale goes that a visiting American, curious about the local drink, was handed a shot of the strong Newfoundland rum. He took a sip and his face instantly contorted in shock at its sharp bite and heat. He let out a loud, screeching cry. From that moment on, the name Screech stuck, and the drink went on to become a Newfoundland tradition.

Although Adrian enjoyed his time at Fort Pepperrell, the routine of office work didn't fully satisfy his ambitions. While he appreciated the camaraderie and the dynamic environment of the base, he longed for something more hands-on, a job that would allow him to connect with the world beyond paperwork and administrative tasks. His exposure to American culture and new ideas at the base inspired him to seek new experiences.

Adrian's Aunt Ella, his mother's sister, was married and living in Buchans, where her husband managed the ASARCO mine. The Buchans mines, operated by the American Smelting and Refining Company (ASARCO), primarily produced lead, zinc, copper, silver, and gold. Aunt Ella and Uncle Edward were very generous to their nieces and nephews. Over the years, they brought several of them to Buchans, offering summer jobs and other forms of assistance. Uncle Edward offered Adrian a job working as a mine timberman assistant, helping to install timber supports in the mine tunnels. Adrian was ready to leave St. John's behind. The prospect of steady employment and a fresh start in Buchans made the decision an easy one for him.

The day Adrian left for Buchans, Junior came with him to the train station to see him off. The brothers promised to keep in touch. Adrian assured Junior he'd be home for Christmas, which seemed to make the goodbye a little easier. This was Adrian's first time travelling alone, and he was excited for the trip.

On the train, he quickly found his berth and settled into a seat by the window. Watching the scenery roll by—forests, ponds, and small towns—soon became his favourite part of the trip. The steady rhythm and slow pace of the train didn't bother him; instead, he enjoyed taking everything in. At each stop, he hopped off to stretch his legs and have a look at what was happening at the station. He especially enjoyed going to the dining car for meals, thinking to himself, "*If Buchans is as good as this, I'm really going to enjoy myself.*"

By the time they reached Millertown Junction, Adrian had struck up conversations with several fellow passengers. As they transferred to the branch line, the train slowed further, weaving its way deeper into the wilderness. The sights became more rugged and remote. Before long, the town seemed to emerge suddenly from the wilderness, revealing a mix of modest houses, company buildings, and dirt roads. Adrian was anxious to meet the locals and get started with his new job.

Adrian liked working in Buchans. He appreciated having a steady job and being part of a tight-knit community. He worked underground helping install and maintain the wooden (and later steel) supports that kept tunnels from collapsing. It was a physically demanding, high-risk job and an essential role in early mining operations. He valued the camaraderie underground, where workers relied on each other in tough, confined conditions.

As a hockey enthusiast, he had worried when he left St. John's that he might not have the opportunity to play again, but those fears were unfounded. Buchans was a hockey town. The Buchans Miners were a powerhouse in the Senior Newfoundland Hockey League, known for their dominance on the ice. In 1948, they became the first Newfoundland senior team to recruit paid players to strengthen their roster. Year after year, the Miners reached the finals and claimed the coveted Herder Trophy multiple times throughout the 1950s, earning them a devoted fan following. As soon as the hockey season was over, Adrian looked forward to softball. He often played shortstop, a position that highlighted his quick reflexes and sharp decision making. One memorable game took place during a local tournament. With two outs in the bottom of the last inning and the bases loaded, Adrian made a diving catch to secure the win. The crowd erupted in cheer, solidifying his reputation as a rock-solid player.

It wasn't just the sports Adrian enjoyed in Buchans; it was also the social life and the strong sense of community spirit. He thrived in the warm gatherings and the friendly atmosphere that made Buchans feel like home. Hardly had he arrived in town before the news spread that a 6'4" handsome new resident was living in the Bunk House. His presence quickly became a topic of conversation. The local girls were particularly taken with Adrian, charmed by his good looks and charismatic personality. He was more than happy to oblige their interest. Adrian had a passion for dancing and made quite an impression on the dance floor. And when the local church called for volunteers to help with the Bingo games, Adrian was quick to step up, selling cards at the door, calling out the numbers and staying afterward to stack the chairs and clean up.

Adrian embraced every aspect of life in Buchans with enthusiasm but he knew there was a bigger world beyond the town—one that would lead him into new places and a different way of living. It was Uncle Edward who first told him about a major project just beginning in the Canadian North. He arranged a job for Adrian there. When word spread that he was leaving, the local hockey club organized a small dinner in his honour. During the evening, two of the young boys he had coached stepped forward and presented him with a small keepsake, offered shyly but with obvious pride. It was a well-worn hockey puck, inscribed with the year and their team's name—a simple gift, but one he could tuck into his bag and carry with him.

EIGHT

The DEW Line

IN THE EARLY 1950s THE DISTANT EARLY WARNING (DEW) Line was being established. The DEW Line was a system of radar stations in the Northern Arctic region of Canada and Greenland. It was an international defence project involving cooperation between the United States, Canada, and other NATO countries set up to detect and provide early warnings of Soviet activity during the Cold War. The DEW Line was arguably the most ambitious and logistically challenging military construction project in Canadian history.

Newfoundland, being strategically located in the North Atlantic, played a significant role in this project as the first few stations were erected in Northern Labrador. During the construction phase of the DEW Line from 1956 to 1958, many Newfoundlanders, including Adrian, were recruited to work on the station sites. In total there were thirty-three stations stretching across 3,600 miles of some of the most desolate and coldest land on earth. There were two types of bases, Main and Auxiliary. The sites were placed approximately 100 miles apart, along the 69th parallel about 200 miles inside the Arctic circle.

Adrian was thrilled to land a job on the DEW Line, though he felt a mix of excitement and nerves—it would be his first time leaving the island. He threw himself into getting ready, picking up all the supplies he'd need and trying to get a sense of what life would be like in such a remote place. He knew he'd miss home, but he was determined to make the most of the opportunity. It seemed like a perfect fit for his interest in travel and exploring new places.

He departed with a group of men on a chartered flight directly to one of the DEW Line bases. From there, he travelled by dog team to his first posting in the Arctic. The vast, frozen landscape seemed to stretch endlessly before him, a stark expanse of silent white broken only by the sound of the dogs' steady paws crunching through the snow and the biting whip of the icy wind against his face. The isolation was profound, and the harshness of the environment was a constant reminder of how unforgiving the wilderness could be.

The dogs, he recalled, were strong, reliable, and up to their task. He admired their resilience and the bond they shared. As they travelled, they encountered fierce blizzards that reduced visibility to near zero and temperatures that cut through even the warmest clothing. Reflecting on it later, Adrian spoke with awe of how the experience tested his endurance, deepened his respect for the land, and strengthened his belief in the teamwork that had carried them through.

He played a key role in the construction phase of the project, where his job was to organize and arrange everything needed to build the various sites. This meant overseeing the transport and setup of essential supplies like food, shelter, tools, machinery, and building materials. These supplies were used to create infrastructure such as buildings, roads, storage tanks, towers, antennas, airfields, and hangars. During the brief Arctic summers, he also handled the tough task of moving materials to different locations, relying on military and civilian airlifts or sealifts to make deliveries to remote Arctic ports.

Selecting sites in Eastern Canada for the DEW Line proved challenging, as the process was hindered by inaccurate or even nonexistent topographic maps. For the Labrador sites, crews were sent out during mid-winter to electronically path test proposed routes. Once a site was chosen, its exact location had to be pinpointed through astronomical surveys, and the terrain mapped topographically. This work took Adrian to some of the most isolated and sparse environments, where he faced extreme weather, isolation, and limited access to amenities.

He worked with radar systems, communications equipment, and other specialized technologies essential for surveillance and defence. This was a key turning point in Adrian's career, expanding his technical knowledge and enhancing his understanding of the crucial systems that played a role in detecting incoming Soviet bombers during the Cold War.

Adrian loved the outdoors and wasn't bothered by the cold at all. He would organize a game of shinny regardless of skill level or weather conditions, using whatever he could find as a stick and improvising a puck from available materials. With just his creativity, he could effortlessly turn a snowy patch into a makeshift hockey rink.

Housing varied from insulated canvas Quonset-type shelters to tents to plywood buildings. The tricks to keeping them habitable were to bank the sides with snow blocks and have a small fan to keep the air from stratifying. The heat came from a kerosene stove. Each sleeping hut had a wash basin. A central wash house took care of showers and laundry. The number of men at each station varied from as few as eight to as many as thirty or forty, depending on the location.

The days were long, but in the evenings, they would gather together and share stories to entertain themselves. Adrian had a particular fondness for a good story. He was an exceptional listener. He quickly learned that everyone had a story to tell and he had a particular knack for drawing these stories out of people, knowing just the right questions to ask to encourage them to open up. His genuine interest and keen listening skills made him a magnet for storytellers, and he relished hearing the diverse experiences and tales from those around him. Some nights, they would gather to play cards. If all the players were Newfoundlanders, they played 120s or Growl as Adrian called it. He was always the first to place a bid and often made the highest bids, usually winning. With alcohol off-limits, they made the most of what was available.

Adrian fondly recalled spending Christmas in the Arctic, a memory that was etched into his heart. The vast whiteness stretched endlessly in every direction, enclosing the world in a serene, almost otherworldly silence. "On Christmas Eve, the stars blazed with an intensity I'd never seen before. As I stood beneath the stars, my thoughts drifted back to the Christmases of my childhood—the stories of the nativity that my mother told me, the image of a humble stable and the miracle of a baby born." In that frozen wilderness, he experienced a quiet, personal epiphany that stayed with him long after the Christmas stars had faded. Facing the cold and the isolation, he understood that he could handle whatever came his way.

NINE

Working with the United Nations

His time working in the Arctic gave Adrian valuable experience and the opportunity to work with people from different cultures as part of a team. This experience broadened his outlook and helped him develop practical skills and lasting connections. Adrian had joined the Military Reservists before leaving St. John's in case other opportunities might arise. In time, these combined experiences led to an opportunity with the United Nations, where he was able to apply what he had learned on a broader stage. While working on the DEW Line, Adrian kept up with his reserve duties back home. One day, he got word that the United Nations was looking for volunteers for a mission overseas. Through the reserves, his name had been passed along, and soon he was being considered for the assignment. It came as a surprise, but also as an exciting opportunity—an unexpected chance to travel and put his skills to use in a very different kind of service.

In 1958, the General Assembly of the United Nations (UN) initiated a project to "employ international machinery for the promotion of the economic and social advancement of all peoples..." as stated in the Charter of the UN. Its operations were intended to speed up the economic development of less-developed countries by creating conditions that facilitated new capital investments of all types. Under this program, countries could apply for assistance to complete various projects aimed at improving their overall social and economic well-being. The initiative would have the resources and capabilities to carry out large-scale projects that required initial investment. The organization kicked off a recruitment campaign aimed at attracting individuals for positions related to technology, telecommunications, and infrastructure development.

As a UN ally, Canada could volunteer Royal Canadian Air Force (RCAF) resources for a UN-led operation or mission whenever it was requested. These missions were usually peacekeeping or peace-related operations. RCAF members serve on UN operations through a formal and structured process within the military construct. Because of his experience and skill set, Adrian was an ideal candidate to volunteer for a position with the UN. He waited many weeks for a reply, and more than once he began to think the answer would never come at all. The selection process was rigorous, thoroughly evaluating his qualifications, operational background, physical fitness, and language abilities. Eventually the reply came.

When Adrian received the letter in response to his application, he was in the high Arctic, enduring long, dark winter days with nearly twenty-four hours of darkness. By then, it had been a while since he'd submitted his application, and he had almost given up on the idea. When he saw he'd been accepted, his immediate thought was, "*It'll be warmer than here, that's for sure!*" Working for the United Nations was an opportunity to make a real difference, even though it came with its fair share of uncertainty. The thought of travelling to new, unfamiliar places and contributing to something bigger than himself sparked a renewed sense of purpose.

He returned to St. John's to prepare for what was ahead. As part of the evaluation process, he was required to spend forty-eight hours in solitary confinement to assess his ability to handle isolation. Adrian's nephew, Johnny, recalled that Adrian got drunk the night before the test and spent the entire forty-eight hours recovering from a hangover. Despite this, he still managed to pass the test with flying colours.

Training for the mission focused on several important skills. It started with basic military exercises, including physical fitness, essential tactics, and jungle survival skills. Participants also learned conflict resolution, negotiation, and peacekeeping to handle disputes effectively. Medical training covered first aid, tropical diseases, and emergency responses. Although he didn't have many details, Adrian knew he was being sent to a part of Africa experiencing political unrest. Intelligence briefings and lessons on the region's political landscape helped the team understand the problems they'd face.

Two of Adrian's former colleagues from the DEW Line were also selected for the project. The three friends made their way to the RCAF base in Winisk, Ontario, for their initial briefing before travelling to New York to begin their orientation. On the flight to New York, Adrian caught the attention of a stewardess, and by the time the plane had landed, he had managed to get her phone number. She and Adrian quickly hit it off and began a whirlwind romance. She took Adrian on a tour of New York, showing him all the city's vibrant sights and sounds. Having spent the past two years in the Arctic, the fast pace of the city and its energy were a thrilling change for Adrian. They enjoyed late-night bars, attended shows, and dined at various restaurants, savouring every new experience. When it was time for Adrian to return, they both wanted to keep in touch. He gave her his mother's address in Brigus South, the best way to reach him, and over the next few months, Maggie received numerous letters and postcards meant for Adrian. She kept them alongside the other letters she had collected over the years from the many women friends Adrian had met along the way.

Following the training period, Adrian and his colleagues were deployed into the field. The first assignment was in what was then commonly referred to as "the Congo," which in 1958 was under Belgian colonial rule. Officially known as the Belgian Congo, it was a territory in Central Africa that had been a Belgian colony since the late nineteenth century. During this time, this part of the Congo was governed directly by Belgium, and the Congolese people had limited political rights and representation. The colonial economy was heavily based on the extraction of natural resources, such as rubber, copper, and other minerals. This exploitation led to significant economic inequality and social unrest among the Congolese people. Congolese leaders and activists were increasingly demanding independence and an end to colonial rule. The political climate in the Congo during this period was tense and increasingly volatile, setting the stage for the events that would lead to its independence as the Republic of Congo on June 30, 1960.

Adrian was part of the UN peacekeeping force tasked with maintaining order and security. This involved patrolling conflict zones, protecting civilians, and ensuring compliance with ceasefire agreements. He took part in delivering food, medical supplies, and other essential resources to communities impacted by conflict or displacement, while also collaborating with local and international organizations to meet urgent needs. His work involved rebuilding roads, schools, hospitals, and water supply systems that had been damaged or neglected due to conflict, and overseeing the coordination of large-scale construction projects. He ensured that resources were allocated efficiently and effectively, striving to restore vital infrastructure and improve the quality of life for affected communities.

The accommodations of the peacekeeping force were simple and practical, reflecting the realities of life in a region with unique hazards. They slept on modest cots, each one draped with mosquito nets—to keep out insects, but also to guard against more dangerous creatures like scorpions, which could slip into their bedding unnoticed. The nets became an essential barrier, providing a small sense of security during long, hot nights. Despite the occasional discomfort, Adrian adjusted to the conditions, knowing that vigilance was a part of everyday life.

There were things Adrian came to love about life in the Congo. For example, during the colonial period, many cities in the Congo had sports clubs founded by both locals and expatriates, and boxing was especially popular. Adrian threw himself into the local boxing scene, quickly building connections within the community. He loved sparring with the locals, picking up techniques fast, and developing a real passion for the sport. Alongside boxing, he worked hard to earn a black belt in judo, a goal that took years of focus and dedication. Training in martial arts built his physical strength and gave him a quiet confidence that stayed with him in every aspect of his life. His time in the Congo, in particular, was a period of real enjoyment and fulfillment. During this time, Adrian learned French, a skill he would continue to use for many years. This experience not only enhanced his professional abilities but also gave him a deep appreciation for languages and the opportunities that come with being able to speak more than one.

After a few years, Adrian took on the role of special liaison, where he was responsible for improving communication and coordination among the various groups involved in the development process. This included collaborating closely with government agencies, local authorities, and international partners to streamline operations and improve teamwork to ensure the success of the projects. His role was key in making sure everyone was aligned and working toward shared goals. Part of Adrian's responsibilities also involved closely monitoring the situation on the ground, documenting human rights abuses, and reporting his findings back to UN headquarters. This information was essential for shaping international policies and response strategies.

Along with his liaison and reporting responsibilities, Adrian took part in reconnaissance missions, which required him to assess and gather intelligence, sometimes in hazardous environments. He moved quietly through villages and along rugged terrain, watching for signs of unrest, noting troop movements, and gathering whatever information he could. During these missions, Adrian worked closely with a specially trained dog named Major, a partner skilled at sniffing out explosives, weapons, or hidden people, and alerting him to potential dangers. The bond between them was strong, with Major's unique skills perfectly suited to the demands of Adrian's work. When Adrian's assignment ended, Major didn't go on another mission. These dogs were trained to work closely with a single handler, and their bond was crucial. Sending them to a new handler could be confusing and stressful, so they usually retired or were put down.

Adrian had always loved dogs. He'd grown up with them around his home in Brigus South. In the Arctic, his respect for them only grew as he saw first-hand how valuable their keen senses, hardiness, and ability to work in extreme cold made them for scouting, tracking, and detecting danger. When he left the UN mission, he missed Major deeply. He longed to know how his loyal companion was doing, but he hesitated to ask. He was unsure if he was ready to hear the answer.

In the early 1960s, Adrian was moved to India. At this time, India was navigating the early years of its independence, having gained freedom from British colonial rule in 1947. Jawaharlal Nehru was the Prime Minister of India. As one of the principal leaders of the Indian independence movement and a close associate of Mahatma Gandhi, Nehru played a crucial role in shaping the newly independent nation. India was implementing its Five-Year Plans, aiming for economic development and industrialization. The government focused on self-sufficiency, building infrastructure, and promoting heavy industries. However, the country struggled with significant issues, including poverty and a lack of modern infrastructure.

The early 1960s were marked by border tensions and conflicts, most notably the Sino-Indian War in 1962, as well as the conflict with China over disputed territories in the Himalayas. Adrian's work in India involved supporting economic-development initiatives, assisting with social reform programs, and promoting education and health care. He was also engaged in peacekeeping and mediation efforts related to regional conflicts and internal disputes, working to foster stability and strength in the areas in which he was involved.

Adrian had dedicated significant time to studying Indian history, developing a deep fascination with Mahatma Gandhi's philosophy of non-violence and his approach to social change. His admiration for Gandhi's ideals led him to form a friendship with an Indian coworker who shared his interest in Gandhi's legacy. Together, they made a pilgrimage to the site of Gandhi's cremation at Raj Ghat in Delhi, a profound experience that allowed

Adrian to connect more deeply with the principles he so admired. He considered himself fortunate to have such a guide, since without him he would not have fully understood the significance of what he was seeing and experiencing. This journey provided Adrian with an even greater understanding of the cultural and historical context in which he worked.

Despite the challenges and demanding nature of his work, Adrian felt a strong sense of fulfillment. He made a point of connecting with the local cultures by immersing himself in their festivals and participating in traditional ceremonies. Adrian later recalled: "One time, I was asked to join a traditional blessing ceremony. I knelt with the others while they said their prayers. It felt a bit strange at first, but there was a quiet calm in the room. Taking part made me feel connected to the people."

Another time, he took part in a welcoming ceremony. Adrian remembered: "It was mostly sharing tea with everyone. Nothing grand, but it was friendly, and it made me feel included in the community." Growing up in Newfoundland, Adrian was used to communities coming together for music, festivals, and shared traditions. Seeing similar ways of connecting in other cultures made him curious, and he spent a lot of time asking questions and learning what these customs meant to the people. He particularly enjoyed those nights when he and his colleagues would sit around in a circle and each person in turn would tell a story or sing a song.

His travels also took him to iconic historical sites, remarkable landmarks, and stunning natural wonders. He particularly enjoyed visiting the ancient temples in India and expansive wildlife reserves in Africa. These experiences allowed him to not only witness the richness of each culture but also to develop a deeper appreciation for their unique histories and ways of life.

While he was away, Adrian regularly sent his cheques home to his mother. Maggie looked forward to her trips to the post office, always hoping to find one of the distinctive blue envelopes that meant a letter from Adrian. In his letters, he detailed his work, sharing stories about the projects he was managing and the tasks he was tackling. He also wrote about the landscapes he explored and the wildlife he encountered.

Knowing his mother would worry, he made sure to include updates on how he was doing in his letters. He told Maggie he was taking care of himself, while getting familiar with new places. He also shared funny stories. He told her about the time he was trying to use more French and had a small mix-up while asking for directions. He thought he had it right, but the man didn't understand him at first then laughed. Adrian had asked about a goat instead of the road. Through his letters, he wanted his mother to know that he was safe and really enjoying his time away.

Maggie always shared the letters with Henry, who took great pleasure in following Adrian's travels. An avid reader with a love of geography, Henry would spread out his old atlas and carefully trace the towns and regions Adrian described.

Adrian spent six years with the United Nations initiative between 1958 and 1964 on assignments in diverse locations across India and Africa. He collaborated closely with engineers, contractors, and local tradespeople. He actively engaged with local communities to understand their needs and ensure the projects met their expectations. As he recalled, "Working in so many places, I realized that the people you meet and the connections you make matter more than any plan or project. Those experiences stayed with me long after I left."

This photo of Adrian, around age 29, was taken while he still worked for the United Nations. Copies were sent to his mother, Uncle Henry, John (Junior), Carmel, and Sheila, to let them know he was doing okay.

Adrian enjoying a rare day off in the Congo. Even amid the demands and responsibilities of his work, he found moments to appreciate the beauty of his surroundings and the experiences that shaped his extraordinary journey.

While exploring Africa, Adrian took particular enjoyment in visiting with the locals and experiencing their heritage and culture.

TEN

Returning to Newfoundland

AS THE PROJECT CAME TO A CLOSE, ADRIAN looked forward to returning home to Newfoundland and reuniting with his family. While his travels had opened his eyes to different ways of life, his strong connection to home remained unchanged. When his plane landed at Torbay Airport, Adrian felt a wave of relief and happiness at being back. After spending much of his twenties away, he returned as a more mature person, shaped by his experiences. Being with his family again brought him comfort as he settled back into familiar routines.

Adrian didn't come back empty-handed. He brought gifts for his family. For his mother, Maggie, he picked out some bright, colourful Congolese fabric and a beautifully carved wooden jewellery box. Maggie adored the box and proudly placed it on the mantle, where it stayed for years, always reminding her of Adrian's time abroad. He also brought back small trinkets for his nieces and nephews, little souvenirs that made them feel included in his travels. As he handed out his gifts, he had a story to go with each one about the people he met and the unique places he visited. It was as if each gift came with a piece of his journey.

One of the first things Adrian did after returning home was to buy a Thunderbird convertible. The car quickly became his pride and joy and a head turner around town. He arranged for the Thunderbird to be specially imported into St. John's, making it one of a kind in the area. The Thunderbird was a showstopper, with its sleek design, powerful V8 engine, and shiny chrome detailing that sparkled in the sunlight. Inside, the leather seats added a touch of luxury. Adrian loved taking the car out for a spin. He was often seen cruising down Water Street with the top down and music blaring. He usually had a companion in tow—a beautiful woman or one of his friends—enjoying the ride as much as he did. The car became a part of his identity, and people in town talked about Adrian and his Thunderbird long after he drove by.

Adrian's mother, now affectionately referred to as Missus Maggie, continued to live in her home in Brigus South with Uncle Henry. While Adrian had been away, life back home had evolved significantly. His brother Junior had married and was raising three children with his wife, also named Sheila, adding a joyful presence to family gatherings. Carmel, now a nurse, had married and settled in St. John's, where she balanced her work at the General Hospital with raising her four children. Adrian delighted in his growing roster of nieces and nephews, embracing the role of the fun uncle who always had a story, joke, or clever remark to share.

Meanwhile, his sister, Sheila, and her husband, Bob McGrath, had established themselves in Port aux Basques, where they co-owned and operated a drugstore. Bob, a trained pharmacist, managed the pharmacy while Sheila played an integral role in running the business. Junior and his wife, Sheila, initially lived in Bay Roberts, but later joined his sister, Sheila, and her husband, Bob, in Port aux Basques, where they welcomed their fourth child. Together, they expanded McGrath's Drugs into a new building, creating space for doctors and dentists to establish practices and serve communities along the rural southwest coast, including several who relocated from England and Ireland to rural Newfoundland. The drugstore became an important service for the smaller communities in the region.

Maggie remained as busy as ever, now with the joy of grandchildren to keep her occupied. She lovingly knitted beautiful mitts and socks for each of them, which became cherished Christmas gifts. Sunday dinner was a special time, served in the middle of the day, with homemade jams, jellies, and pickles always on the table. The kettle was always ready for tea, and friends and family knew they were welcome to stop by. Everyone enjoyed sitting around the table, sharing stories, and catching up.

The family remained close, frequently visiting each other and spending time together in Brigus South. Adrian also shared a special relationship with his nieces and nephews. They have vivid memories of his visits, when he would arrive laden with all sorts of things they weren't usually allowed. He delighted in breaking small rules, piling them into his convertible for long drives that inevitably included stops he insisted were "just between us"—bags of candy and bottles of drink. He'd wink and tell them not to say a word, though he knew full well they would. Whether circling the long way home or letting them sit up front and choose the music, he had a knack for making each of them feel special. As they grew older, they stayed close to him, seeking his advice and respecting his wisdom well into their adult years.

During this time, Adrian often travelled back and forth between St. John's and Brigus South, enjoying the chance to spend time with his mother and Uncle Henry. Uncle Henry had given up his dream of living in New York and returned home after Adrian's father passed away, stepping in to help the family during a tough time. Instead of seeing this as a sacrifice, Henry accepted it without complaint and carried on with quiet dignity. Uncle Henry's strength had a lasting impact on their lives. He never complained, criticized, or got involved in discipline, always leaving that to Maggie. Though he was aware of everything around him, he never spoke out of turn. As they got older, Adrian and his siblings made sure Uncle Henry knew how much they loved and appreciated him, often going out of their way to show their gratitude.

When Adrian suggested they drive across Newfoundland together, Uncle Henry was all for it. The prospect of exploring the island intrigued him, especially since Sheila and Bob were living in Port aux Basques. Driving across Newfoundland in 1964 would have taken a considerable amount of time due to the condition of the roads and the limited infrastructure. The Trans-Canada Highway, which connects the island from east to west, was still under construction. Depending on the route taken and the conditions of the roads, it could have taken several days to complete the journey.

Adrian and Henry cut a striking figure as they set out together, both tall and slim, good-looking, and with full heads of hair. The long drive gave them plenty of time to catch up; Adrian talked about his life in the Congo while Henry talked about his time in New York. It was the first time they had spent so many hours alone together and they discovered things about each other they hadn't known before. At one point, Henry told Adrian about a time in New York when he had felt completely alone, and for the first time, Adrian heard the loneliness Henry had kept to himself. His respect for his uncle only grew.

When they rolled into Port aux Basques in the convertible with the top down, they couldn't help but turn heads. They spent a few fun days with Bob and Sheila, meeting friends, and checking out the town. They had such a great time that Sheila decided to tag along on the ride back to St. John's, bringing her young son, Keith, with her.

After returning from his travels, Adrian wasted no time reconnecting with his old friends and meeting new people. He visited familiar haunts in St. John's, catching up with acquaintances and immersing himself once again in the local social scene. Shortly after his return, he was introduced to Dr. Barry Martin and his wife, Lois. Barry had come to Newfoundland from Ireland as a young doctor. Shortly after his arrival, he met and married a local girl, Lois Mills, and they had just taken up residence in Ferryland, where Barry worked as a family practitioner. Barry and Adrian became fast friends. Barry and Lois's house was always full of music, friends, and young people. Adrian thrived in this environment.

Barry and Adrian would often find themselves engaged in deep conversations that stretched long into the night, delving into a wide range of subjects, from history and politics to poetry and philosophy. Adrian's passion for history had taken root during his time in the Arctic, where one of his colleagues, an Irish man, had brought along a collection of Irish history and literature. The long, quiet nights in the remote environment provided the perfect opportunity for Adrian to immerse himself in these works, igniting a profound interest in Irish history. This was similar to his time in the Congo, where he had expanded his historical studies to include African history, driven by his curiosity about the diverse cultures and complex political landscapes he encountered.

Barry, too, was a history enthusiast, with a wealth of knowledge and an impressive library that spanned a variety of topics. They often exchanged books, recommending titles they thought the other might enjoy or learn from. They would take turns recounting stories from their own lives too. These exchanges allowed them to challenge each other's perspectives. Their discussions often turned into spirited debates, with each trying to defend their viewpoints or push the other to think more critically.

Adrian's tales transported listeners to the depths of the Congo, painting vivid pictures of dense jungles and exotic creatures. He had the ability to captivate people and spin yarns that he embellished depending on the situation. In a community renowned for its talented storytellers, Adrian stood out as a masterful one. He adhered to the old adage: never let the truth get in the way of a good story. His tales were a constant source of entertainment and wonder, leaving his audience eagerly anticipating what he would come up with next. He shared many extraordinary experiences, but not all were lighthearted. In particular, he would recount the unsettling scenes of public executions he had witnessed, which deeply disturbed him, and lingered in his memory long after he'd left. As he said, "different cultures have their own ways of doing things, even if some of them were hard for me to accept."

Barry and Adrian enjoyed hopping in the car and driving down the Southern Shore to visit friends and acquaintances. Between the two of them, they knew just about everyone, or at least most of the families in the area. It was common for them to stop by for a surprise visit and be welcomed with warmth. People were happy to offer them a drink and good company. Both men took great pleasure in spending time with ordinary folks, feeling most comfortable in relaxed settings like a local kitchen, where they could have honest conversations and share a laugh. Many of these visits ended in Maggie's kitchen in Brigus South where Barry would leave with a jar of homemade jam or pickles to take home.

On one occasion, Barry brought along his Irish wolfhound. While he and Adrian were inside the house having a cup of tea, the dog found its way into the neighbour's henhouse. Before long the hens were squawking and scattering in every direction, feathers flying as complete pandemonium broke out. The neighbours, who had never seen a dog like this before, came running as soon as they heard the commotion, shouting and trying to chase the dog away while gathering their frantic hens. Although a few feathers and eggs were lost in the chaos, most of the hens were eventually rounded up and returned to the coop.

Maggie had just gotten her first television set, though she had mixed feelings about it. She'd always loved her radio, which was constantly on in the background. The television, though, seemed like a bit of an extravagance to her, something she wasn't sure they really needed. Adrian would torment her about her hesitation. He'd tease her about being "fancy" now, joking that she'd forget all about her radio with her new "window to the world." He'd go on about how she might end up glued to it all day. Maggie would laugh and shake her head, insisting that nothing could replace her trusty old radio.

Adrian had returned to Newfoundland with a hard-earned black belt in judo, and was thrilled to discover that a judo club had opened in St. John's. He soon became a fixture at the club where he'd downplay his experience, saying, "Oh, I just know a few basics." When people asked about his time training abroad, he'd brush it off with a laugh, insisting, "It's nothing you couldn't pick up in a good snowball fight here!" When offering advice to beginners, he kept it simple, reminding them that judo was not just about technique but about its values—courage, respect, modesty, friendship, and honour.

Before long Adrian was looking for a new job. The province had just announced its first major publicly owned hydroelectric project at Bay d'Espoir. The project was built to provide low-cost power, which would help extend the island's utility services and provide an incentive to attract new industries.

Premier Smallwood, ever keen on fostering industrial growth, viewed this venture as a significant step towards achieving his economic vision for the province. He launched the project with great fanfare, ensuring it received the attention and support necessary for its success. Located on the south coast of Newfoundland, Bay d'Espoir taps into a watershed with large lakes, and a significant river system, including the Salmon, Grey, and White Bear. The area's rugged terrain and abundant natural resources made it an ideal site for such an ambitious endeavour, with the potential to provide substantial power for the region. The project not only promised to boost the local economy, but also offered new opportunities for development and growth in the surrounding communities.

There was a lot of buzz about the new venture and the jobs it would bring. Smallwood promoted it with plenty of fanfare. Adrian learned they were looking for an experienced manager to oversee the construction phase, and after a single phone call, the position was his. He was twenty-nine years old, with a surprising amount of experience already under his belt. He had seen and done more than many men twice his age, but the road was long and full of possibilities; he felt ready for whatever came next.

ELEVEN

The Accident

THE ENGINEERING WORK BEGAN IN APRIL 1964, and the main construction a year later. Adrian set off from St. John's in his Classic Jeep CJ-5, ready for his role as a manager on the project. The rugged, four-wheel-drive vehicle was perfect for navigating the tough terrain he would encounter on the way to the site. The drive itself was long, with few places to stop, little signage, and few vehicles to pass along the way.

Construction of the road linking Bay d'Espoir to Bishop's Falls began in the mid 1960s alongside development of the hydro project. The highway was not completed until 1967. Once Adrian passed Bishop's Falls, there was no direct highway. Adrian would likely have followed existing gravel logging roads, local secondary routes, and whatever rough links connected toward the Bay d'Espoir area along the north side of the bay. Much of the journey was over dirt roads, with dust clouds kicked up behind his vehicle. He navigated around potholes, sharp turns, and uneven stretches, all while surrounded by nothing but wilderness.

Upon arriving at Bay d'Espoir, Adrian was greeted by a raw, undeveloped landscape—a vast stretch of rocky terrain, dense forests, and the rough outline of the coast. Construction vehicles and machinery were scattered around, marking the beginnings of a worksite just starting to take shape.

Adrian's role involved supervising the construction of dams, spillways, penstocks, and other essential structures for hydroelectric power generation. He established living quarters at Camp Boggy, which became the central hub for the project. Adrian lived in one of the staff houses on site. Camp Boggy accommodated twenty-five families and included living quarters, dining areas, administrative offices and a few recreational facilities for the residents.

Living in these close quarters fostered a sense of camaraderie among the workers. They worked hard all week, enduring long hours and tough conditions, but on weekends, they relaxed and let loose. Adrian often took charge of organizing gatherings. There were parties with music every Saturday night. Often, one of Adrian's coworkers played guitar, and Adrian would try his best to keep the beat. Timing wasn't always his strong suit, but if you needed someone who knew all the words, Adrian was your guy, singing along with enthusiasm to everything from country songs to classic folk ballads.

Adrian threw himself into his work at Bay d'Espoir, determined to master every aspect and keep things running smoothly. He enjoyed being part of a team and formed strong friendships with his coworkers. Being back in Newfoundland, surrounded by familiar landscapes and faces made him happy.

One of his favourite ways to unwind was salmon fishing on the Conne River. Adrian often went with a fellow worker who shared his love of fishing, and they would spend hours by the river, casting lines in silence, enjoying the quiet and the scenery. They usually lit a fire and cooked a meal, with Adrian always bringing his kettle for tea. In the winter, he liked to strap on snowshoes and take long walks, revelling in the stillness of the surroundings. Being back in Newfoundland felt right, and he found peace in the natural beauty around him.

Less than two years after he started the job, Adrian was involved in a terrible accident that ended his career and almost took his life. Adrian was driving his own vehicle across a temporary bridge on the construction site, when it gave way beneath the truck, sending it into the water. While the other two occupants in the vehicle suffered only minor injuries, Adrian's spinal cord was severed. He was brought to the hospital in St. John's in critical condition.

According to his nephew, Johnny, it was the gleam from Adrian's watch that helped rescuers locate him. Watches had always been a quiet passion of his; over the years he had collected many during his travels, and he delighted in giving them to those he cared about. In that moment, a small piece of his personality—his love of watches—had quite literally helped save him.

For a week or so, he teetered between life and death. His mother, Maggie, sisters Sheila and Carmel, and brother Junior were at his side. The initial course of treatment was to try and stabilize his condition and address any complications as they arose. Adrian had suffered a complete spinal cord injury at the cervical level, meaning there was complete paralysis below the point of injury. All sensory, motor, and autonomic function below the neck stopped. He remained in critical condition for several weeks. Throughout this period, he suffered two heart attacks and four respiratory collapses, with doctors offering little hope for his survival.

Despite the grim prognosis, Adrian's excellent physical condition saved him. His immediate care focused on stabilizing his medical condition, addressing other injuries, and implementing measures to manage pain, as well as prevent infections and maintain proper respiratory function. In the weeks that followed, he received support from a multidisciplinary medical team including physicians, nurses, physical therapists, and other specialists. They worked together to provide the best possible care and support for his recovery. Adrian's friend Dr. Barry Martin wasted no time visiting him and offering both his medical expertise and emotional support. Barry provided valuable insights and advocated for specific treatments or interventions he believed would benefit Adrian's recovery. His presence brought great comfort to the family during a difficult time.

Years later, Adrian recounted the events of those few days:

> It was an icy cold evening. We were driving back to camp—the timbers gave way and I was thrown out of the truck into the water. I could feel a burning sensation in my neck and jaw and then darkness overtook me. I woke up and could hear humming and buzzing, noises of machines. I could feel something in my throat—I wanted to reach up and take it out but I couldn't. I remember my lips were dry and they hurt. I couldn't keep my eyes open and I couldn't lift my head. I would drift back and forth into darkness. I was burning up—I remember the nurse wiping my forehead with a cool cloth and then I could hear my mother crying.

Adrian continued:

> Mother, Junior, Sheila, and Carmel all kept asking me to wake up. I realized I was in hospital but couldn't remember how I got there. I drifted into darkness again and felt my body become very light. I felt the presence of angels as they directed me toward a bright light. I didn't know if it was the sun or not but I felt myself gently floating towards it. I could look down

> and see my body on the bed. I could see my mother praying and I could see the priest as well. I was being anointed and could hear the prayers of all my family. I felt at peace—nothing was hurting and I felt free from the machines. Then I heard my mother saying, "Please God, don't take him from us, there's a place in heaven for him but not just yet."

Hearing his mother's prayers stirred a mix of emotions in Adrian, and he later said they gave him the strength to persevere through his recovery.

Coming to terms with the physical effects of quadriplegia was a gradual and extremely painful process for Adrian. Adjusting to the significant changes in mobility, independence, and daily life was emotionally and psychologically demanding. As he described to his niece, Jeanine:

> In the weeks following my accident, I became aware of my surroundings and also my limitations. I was keenly aware that I had survived a heart attack and they had lost me for a few minutes. I wanted to tell my mother about the moment when I saw the angels but I wasn't confident that she would understand. I kept the knowledge of that moment when they had lost me to myself but often called upon it when the struggle got too great.

After Adrian was stabilized, a rehabilitation team including doctors, nurses, physiotherapists, and occupational therapists began working to help him modify and regain as much function as possible. Over the course of eight months, he underwent an intensive rehabilitation program tailored to address the changes in his body and to help him rebuild his independence.

The rehabilitation program initially centred on what Adrian could actively do to maintain his health, prevent complications, and preserve as much independence as possible, given that he had very limited movement below the neck. A caregiver or therapist would guide him through carefully designed exercises targeting specific muscle groups, performing passive range-of-motion routines to keep his joints flexible and prevent stiffness or contractures. Because his spinal cord injury reduced his lung capacity, he was also taught breathing exercises to strengthen his lungs, improve oxygen flow, and lower the risk of respiratory infections such as pneumonia.

After eight months, Adrian's doctors decided to send him to Queen Mary Veteran's Hospital in Montreal, which was known for its excellent services for people with spinal cord injuries. They believed the hospital's specialized facilities and access to more resources could give Adrian better treatment options and support. Arrangements were made to transport Adrian by air ambulance, ensuring he was safe and comfortable throughout the trip. This service also allowed him to get the medical care he needed as soon as he arrived in Montreal.

It was the spring of 1967, but St. John's was still buried in deep snowbanks. The day he left, a snowstorm swept through the city as if winter was unwilling to let go. Looking back, Adrian often spoke about the deep loneliness he felt when the decision was made that he should leave the province. Although he was hopeful about the opportunities ahead, the transition was incredibly hard. His mother was there at the hospital to say goodbye, and he talked with his brother, Junior, who, more than anyone else understood what he was feeling.

Once settled at Queen Mary Hospital, Adrian slept in a regular bed for the first time since his accident. Prior to this, he had been confined to a striker frame, in which he lay flat and was turned from his back to his stomach every two hours. Days stretched on as he stared at the ceiling or the floor, his view limited to tiles, cracks, or the faint shadows cast by the room's lights. Despite receiving excellent care in St. John's, he had developed bed sores, which required immediate attention. Skin grafts were performed on the bed sores as well as the tracheotomy site and an intensive physiotherapy program followed.

Adrian entertained himself by imagining shapes in the cracks on his hospital room ceiling. He'd picture the way light and shadow danced across them, forming patterns similar to a spider's web. He envisioned a hockey rink and placed himself at left wing, gliding effortlessly across the ice. In his mind's eye, he could hear the crowd's roar, feel the chill of the rink, and see the puck sliding toward him. For a brief time, he could escape the confines of his reality and immerse himself in the thrill of the game. However, as vivid as these daydreams were, they also served as a poignant reminder of the challenges he faced.

He spent eighteen months at Queen Mary Hospital. It was 1967 and Expo 67, the landmark international exhibition to commemorate Canada's hundredth birthday, was happening. The buzz was exhilarating and palpable. Despite being confined to his hospital room, Adrian could sense the excitement and anticipation radiating from the city. He was angry. He was thirty minutes away from the world's greatest party yet couldn't participate. Seeing and hearing about others enjoying the celebrations intensified his sense of isolation—a stark reminder of his physical limitations.

During this time, several family members travelled from Newfoundland to visit. While their main reason was to see him, they also took the opportunity to enjoy many of the Expo 67 events. Adrian couldn't help but feel left out. Some of his frustration was aimed at his own limitations, but he also felt that their trip was more about experiencing Expo 67 than spending time with him. He couldn't shake the feeling that he was an afterthought or that visiting him was a way to justify their trip.

It was at this time that he started to question why so much energy and funding went into events like Expo 67 while progress in areas like rehabilitation seemed slow. He felt frustrated, thinking society cared more about big celebrations than providing essential services for people who really needed them. During his recovery, he had a lot of time to think. He started to feel that society's resources could be put to better use solving important social issues. As he said to his brother, "Why celebrate with grandeur when we are neglecting the basic needs of those who truly require help?" Looking back, Adrian recognized that his time of reflection was what inspired him to take up advocacy work later on.

TWELVE

Moving to the Hoyles Home

AFTER SPENDING EIGHTEEN MONTHS IN MONtreal, Adrian's medical team concluded that they had exhausted all available treatment options and further intervention was unlikely to improve his condition. He was discharged and arrangements were made to bring him back to Newfoundland. His family explored rehabilitation services outside of hospital as he adjusted to this new phase of his life. After almost two years of intense treatment, the only movement he had below his neck was in his right hand. Although he was unable to grip anything, he was able to operate electronic equipment, including an electric wheelchair. However, at the time he was provided with only a manual wheelchair.

Getting Adrian back to Newfoundland took careful planning to make sure he was safe and comfortable during the trip. He was given a special wheelchair when he was discharged, and the airline made arrangements to meet his mobility needs. Transportation and a place to stay in St. John's were also organized. Adrian was brought to the Sanatorium on Topsail Road, known as "the san." Built in 1917, it had been the main place for treating tuberculosis in Newfoundland. By the late 1960s, it no longer housed TB patients and was used for other purposes, including caring for people in transition—those recovering from illness or waiting for placement elsewhere and those who, for a time, simply had nowhere else to go and needed care and a place to stay. Adrian arrived there in late 1968 and stayed for several months while waiting for a more permanent place to live.

Returning to Newfoundland marked a major turning point in Adrian's life. He had left for Montreal filled with hope and optimism, but coming home signalled that nothing more could be done medically. Facing the reality of a permanent disability was deeply emotional and challenging, forcing him to mourn the loss of his physical abilities and independence. What about the future he had envisioned for himself? The initial shock was overwhelming.

One moment, he was living a life of familiar routines, and the next he was confronted with the harsh truth that things would never be the same. He had to grapple with the loss of abilities that had once been central to his identity. Simple activities like walking, running, skating, dancing, driving, even tasks like caring for his personal hygiene suddenly became impossible on his own. It wasn't just the physical losses that hurt—it was the independence and freedom they represented. Relying on others for things he once did effortlessly was a blow to his pride and self-esteem.

The life Adrian had imagined seemed to collapse, leaving him to navigate an uncharted and difficult path. Accepting this new reality was a slow and painful process, requiring patience, resilience, and a gradual search for meaning in his altered circumstances. The change brought overwhelming feelings of despair and loneliness. His physical limitations were a constant reminder of all he had lost, and the weight of that loss seemed to permeate every aspect of his life. He felt isolated, as though no one could fully grasp the depth of his struggle or the emotional toll of his journey.

His relationships with family and friends became strained, as his struggles made it hard for him to connect with them the way he once had. He worked to find the motivation to do even the simplest things, and the future felt hopeless. He found himself in a constant battle between wanting to move forward and being buried in grief and despair. Adrian felt trapped in a cycle of suffering. At his lowest point, the pain became unbearable, and he reached a place where even the thought of continuing seemed impossible. In a moment of extreme vulnerability, he turned to his brother and begged him to turn off the machine that was keeping him alive. It wasn't just about the physical pain—it was a desperate cry for peace, a wish for an end to the emotional torment that had taken over his life. His brother, resolute in his love for Adrian, stayed by his side through those dark moments. Slowly, with the help of his family and friends, he came to realize that even in the worst of times, there were still moments of connection, meaning, and hope. These sparks kept him going. They helped show him that recovery, though long and difficult, was possible.

Coming to terms with living with a permanent disability was incredibly painful for Adrian, but it also opened the door to finding new ways to live. Barry Martin was a steady source of encouragement, constantly reassuring him that everything would eventually work out. One piece of advice Barry gave him made a lasting impression: "You've only got your head to make a living, so you better figure out how to use it."

Depression is a common issue for people in Adrian's situation and the resources and support available to him, especially in an institutional setting, were scarce. Confronting the depths of his depression felt overwhelming. When his family and friends realized the extent of his struggle, they rallied around him. Although they often felt powerless to change his circumstances, their presence, encouragement, and advocacy became a lifeline for Adrian. His mother visited frequently, and her presence brought Adrian rare moments of calm and relief. Having his hair combed was one of the few physical comforts Adrian truly enjoyed. Maggie, Sheila, and Carmel would sit for hours, gently combing his hair while they talked about the ordinary events of the day. Getting through his deep depression was a tough and slow process, but the love and support of his family and friends made a big difference.

In early 1969, Adrian was transferred to the Hoyles Home on Portugal Cove Road in St. John's. It became his home for the rest of his life (with the exception of three years spent in Halifax). The Hoyles Home was a residential facility for individuals with physical and intellectual disabilities providing a range of services including housing, medical care, and rehabilitation programs. At the Hoyles Home, Adrian was allocated a private room, despite the regular rooming arrangement being four persons per room. This was the first bit of good news he had heard in a while.

With the stability of a private room and a supportive environment, Adrian now had the opportunity to consider his future path. In Montreal, he had started seriously thinking about the issues that persons with disabilities faced. He thought about ways he might help in this area. As he said himself, he no longer had his physical faculties, so he had to focus on his mental and intellectual capacity. He decided he would apply to university to complete undergraduate studies with the plan of eventually studying law. He knew that being quadriplegic would make university life difficult. In 1969, accessibility for individuals with disabilities was limited everywhere, not just on university campuses. On top of that, societal attitudes created additional barriers, making full participation in an academic environment difficult. Despite these obstacles, Adrian applied to Memorial University and was accepted to start in the fall of 1969. Now, to figure out how to make it all work.

His friends and family helped him come up with a plan. There was a lot to sort out, like how to pay for tuition and what kind of support he'd need for his studies. Everyone chipped in with ideas and suggestions. To help cover the costs, the Adrian Battcock Rehabilitation Fund was set up in Cape Broyle, with Barry Martin taking charge of the fundraising efforts. Barry quickly got to work organizing a big benefit concert in St. John's to raise money for a much-needed electric wheelchair. Known for being a great friend to Irish newcomers in Newfoundland, Barry often opened his home to those settling into their new lives. This time, he reached out to a group of these performers, asking them to lend their talents to help Adrian. They were eager to pitch in. The concert took place at the Arts and Culture Centre in St. John's and featured the Irish band Sullivan's Gypsies. Barry and Lois Martin took on the task of running the event from start to finish, overseeing every aspect of it. They leveraged the power of their network of friends, family, and colleagues in coordinating logistics, spreading the word, and selling tickets.

Lois poured hours into hand painting each poster before putting them up around town. She picked high-traffic spots, making sure they'd catch people's eyes and draw them in. Meanwhile, Barry was on the phone constantly, calling up everyone he knew and dropping off tickets all over St. John's. He made it personal, showing up at people's doors with tickets in hand and a big smile, making sure they felt included. Their dedication was the heart and soul of the event's success. It wasn't just about getting things done—it was clear that, for both of them, this project was a labour of love, and they were determined to see it thrive.

Their planning paid off as the concert completely sold out. The evening turned out to be an incredible success, raising significant funds and bringing the audience together in a great sense of community spirit. Adrian and his sister Carmel sat proudly in the front row of the theatre and were delighted with the outcome. When Carmel wheeled Adrian onto the stage, he was met with thunderous applause. He took the opportunity to express his thanks to everyone involved in organizing the event and to the audience for their support.

Just a couple of weeks later, the stage was set once again, this time in Ferryland for a repeat event. Again, the community gathered for an evening of music, camaraderie, and support. Three performers at the concerts, Dermot O'Reilly, Fergus O' Byrne, and Denis Ryan, went on to form the group Ryan's Fancy, which became a household name in Newfoundland and left an indelible mark on the musical landscape of the province. Barry and Lois hoped the benefit concert would raise enough funds to buy an electric wheelchair, and they were delighted when their efforts achieved exactly that.

Adrian and his sister Sheila McGrath, visiting him at the Hoyles Home. Visits like these were always treasured occasions, bringing laughter, conversation, and the warmth of being with family.

During his years at Mount Cashel, Robert (Rob) McGrath became a close friend of Adrian and Junior, but he officially became part of the Battcock family when he married their younger sister, Sheila. After graduating from Mount Cashel, Robert pursued studies in pharmacy and went on to enjoy a long and successful career in his chosen profession.

THIRTEEN

University Life

WITH THE SUCCESS OF THE FUNDRAISERS behind him, Adrian felt more motivated than ever to push ahead with his plans. He arranged a tour of the Memorial University campus before classes started. The visit was a real eye-opener. He was both surprised and disappointed to find the campus filled with obstacles; steps, narrow hallways, and inaccessible entrances made it impossible for him to get around independently. Concerned that these barriers might put his plans at risk, he reached out to the university administration, hoping they could accommodate him. However, the response was discouraging: they explained that the campus facilities were simply not equipped for the changes he needed, and there was little they could do to help. It was a tough blow, making him wonder if his dreams of attending university might be slipping away.

Adrian told his brother about a hurtful remark made by someone in the Registrar's office: "You need to be able to write to attend classes, so if you can't write, you can't attend Memorial University." Hearing this hit him hard. Already feeling nervous about whether he could handle navigating the university, this comment only deepened his doubts and fears. The words lingered, sticking with Adrian in a way that shaped how he saw himself and his abilities, making him second-guess whether his dream of attending university was truly within reach.

However, Adrian wasn't one to back down. He contacted various media outlets to share his story. The media picked up the story generating conversations about accessibility and the rights of individuals with disabilities. It led to a thought- provoking discussion when it was featured on a local call-in talk show. As listeners tuned in to hear diverse perspectives on the issue, the phone lines lit up with callers voicing their opinions. Some callers expressed support for Adrian and called for greater inclusivity, while others expressed resistance to the idea of investing resources in making environments more accessible, citing cost concerns. Some argued that individuals with disabilities should simply make do with existing structures rather than expect accommodations be made for them. Understandably, Adrian was disappointed by the community's response.

He also knew that his mother, Maggie, who would be listening to the program in Brigus South, would be extremely upset by the callers' attitudes and the fact that they would be discussing her son on the radio. For a family that cherished their privacy, this was too much. This upset him even more. Feeling frustrated by the lack of progress and the resistance from the university administration, Adrian decided to take a more unconventional approach that would force them to listen. On the day of registration, he called an ambulance and arranged with some of his friends to be left on a stretcher outside the door of the Registrar's office. On his jacket was a note stating that he would continue to do this everyday until he was admitted. The following day he was admitted as a student at Memorial University.

Hasty, improvised arrangements were made to give Adrian access to the buildings, including a makeshift ramp and other temporary adjustments. These quick fixes were far from perfect and only showed how lacking the campus was in proper accessibility, making it clear that real solutions were needed. Adrian's story of getting admitted became legendary on campus. Some students even joked that the Registrar kept a special stretcher just for him in case he ever needed to make another dramatic entrance. Adrian's experience made it clear that there was a real need for more awareness and advocacy when it came to disability rights. He resolved to confront the barriers in his own life directly, while also advocating for more inclusive spaces not only at the university, but in the wider community. He emphasized the urgency of implementing these changes without delay. Adrian is on record as saying, "these improvements can't be just quick fixes—they are essential for creating an environment where everyone can feel included and supported."

He continued to rally support. He organized a group of student volunteers who assisted him with tasks like taking notes during lectures and carrying his books. With their help, he felt more determined to continue advocating for a better, more accessible university. He stayed in touch with teachers and administrators, regularly sharing his concerns and offering ideas for improvements. Adrian knew that change wouldn't happen overnight. He knew that real progress takes time and hard work, and he was ready to do his part. Despite challenges with accessibility, Adrian got fully involved in student life at Memorial. He made use of support services and accommodations to help him get around campus and connect with other students, making the most of his time there.

Adrian's days started early, since he needed a lot of help before he could even think about heading to the university. From the moment he woke up, his caregivers helped him with everything—bathing, dressing, and preparing for the day ahead. Although the process was time-consuming and demanding, Adrian maintained his sense of humour, often joking that he had become an expert in delegation. He guided his caregivers with a cheerful attitude, always accompanied by a smile and a quick wit.

After his accident, Adrian's senses became heightened, a phenomenon that is well documented. His hearing became remarkably sharp; he could recognize the footsteps of nurses and caregivers, identifying them by the way they walked or how they opened the door. He became attuned to subtle sounds, like the ticking of a watch or the hum of the elevator, to such a degree that he could tell the exact time without even looking at a clock.

His sense of smell also became exceptionally strong. He could identify people by their scent—whether it was the cologne or perfume they wore, the faint trace of cigarette smoke, or the absence of it. He could tell which attendants didn't smoke, as most of the staff were regular smokers. He became especially sensitive to the smells of food, able to tell what meals were being prepared by the scents drifting through the Home. The familiar smells of the outdoors, like the fresh air after a heavy rain or the scent of lilacs in the early summer, felt more intense than before.

His sense of touch, too, became heightened. He continued to find comfort in the simple act of having someone comb his hair, feeling each gentle stroke with a new level of sensitivity. He especially enjoyed the sensations of the outdoors—the feel of rain, snow, or the wind on his face. The wind, in particular, was something he cherished, as it seemed to connect him more deeply with the world around him.

Although his field of vision was restricted by his limited range of motion, he found he noticed things he might have missed before, like the subtle changes in light or the way the shadows fell across the gardens, adding a new layer of richness to his environment.

Since there wasn't a wheelchair-accessible vehicle available at the Hoyles Home, his caregivers came up with a practical solution: they used a specially made transfer board. They would carefully lift him onto the board, and from there he would slide across into the taxi seat. It wasn't always easy, but with careful coordination between the caregivers and taxi drivers, they made sure Adrian could travel safely and comfortably. This setup became a reliable way for Adrian to get where he needed to go.

Gulliver's Taxi was the company Mount Cashel usually called when transportation was needed and before long Adrian came to know several of the drivers by name. In the cars there was always the thick, lingering smell of cigarette smoke that seemed to cling to the upholstery no matter the season. The drivers smoked constantly. A cigarette would rest between a driver's fingers as he steered with one hand, the window cracked open an inch. Now and then, one of them would offer Adrian a cigarette too. Because he could not hold it himself, the driver would place it between his lips and light it for him, then hold it there when his hands were needed on the wheel. The rides were easy and unhurried. They talked about ordinary things—weather, hockey scores, small happenings around town. The drivers told stories about late-night fares and roadside mishaps, and Adrian answered with stories of his own. Those taxi drivers brought new voices and faces into his life.

When Adrian arrived on campus, he had to figure out how to get around the different classrooms and buildings. Luckily, he had his group of supportive friends. They walked with him between classes, making sure he could get through crowded hallways safely. These friendships, along with meaningful relationships with some faculty, helped Adrian feel he truly belonged at the university. Their support was steady, but the atmosphere on campus was not always entirely welcoming. In 1970, people with disabilities were still largely invisible in public life, and Adrian's presence unsettled some. There were quiet murmurs about special arrangements —extra time, modified access, or the assistance he required.

A welcome gift at this time was a compact cassette recorder which allowed him to record his lectures with greater independence. The recorder was designed with an easy-touch stop/start button, which required only a single finger to operate. This small feature made a huge difference for Adrian, who could now control the device with minimal effort. Taping lectures became an essential part of his study routine, though it was still a painstaking process for him. Despite the effort required, this device opened up new possibilities for learning, giving him a way to review and retain information that might otherwise have been difficult to capture in real time.

Before long, Adrian's friends were making tapes of his favourite music. When the elevator doors opened on his floor, the sound of music often greeted visitors, adding a sense of energy and vibrancy to the otherwise quiet surroundings. Some residents weren't as enthusiastic, occasionally grumbling about the volume or the late hours when Adrian's playlist stretched into the night. Adrian, however, wasn't overly concerned with the occasional complaints. For him, the music was a way to keep his spirit alive.

Due to his personal needs, Adrian had to return to the Hoyles Home after three or four hours each day. This routine significantly impacted his ability to follow the traditional academic schedule. Unlike most students, who enrolled in five courses per semester, Adrian's limited time on campus made it impossible for him to maintain such a course load. Instead, he adapted by attending university across three semesters each year, maximizing his available time. This meant that he was able to keep up with his coursework and make steady progress. His hard work paid off. He finished all the requirements for his degree in just four years, right on schedule with the rest of his classmates.

Throughout Adrian's entire time at university, there is no record of him in any official student publications like *The Muse* or *Luminus*, nor in the minutes of student council meetings. This absence is striking, especially considering he was the first quadriplegic student to enroll and he had many issues to deal with, from being accepted as a student to navigating the physical barriers of campus life. His struggles and achievements went unrecognized, both socially and institutionally, reflecting a broader neglect of people with disabilities during that time.

Adrian's story highlights a troubling gap in how narratives are documented and shared. His determination and resilience, despite physical obstacles and feelings of exclusion were significant, but remained invisible in official accounts. This lack of acknowledgement underscores how the contributions and experiences of people with disabilities have often been marginalized, denying them the recognition they deserve. Including stories like Adrian's is essential for creating a fuller, more inclusive account of history—one that reflects the experiences of everyone, not just those who fit traditional moulds.

FOURTEEN

A Special Friend

WHILE ADRIAN WAS IN MONTREAL, HE HAD a special visitor from home. Regina Sullivan, who had grown up in Calvert, not far from Brigus South, came to visit him. Their families had known each other for many years, and although Regina was younger than Adrian, she remembered him from growing up. He was friendly with her older brother and she had seen him play hockey. She had quietly carried a youthful crush on him, though she never imagined he would have noticed her at the time. When she heard about the accident, she was deeply shaken and felt compelled to help. She made the trip to Montreal to see him. She had expected to see Adrian as she remembered him—strong, confident, and full of life, but the reality of his situation hit her hard. It was a lot to process. Despite the shock she felt, the old affection returned, no longer a childish crush but something deeper and steadier. She stayed in contact with him, and when he returned to St. John's, she was there, ready to help.

At the time, Regina was working as a registered nurse in St. John's, which meant she could offer practical advice about his recovery. She was also someone he could talk to and trust. Sometimes she shared what she knew about rehabilitation; other times she simply listened. Her visit reassured him and made him feel less alone. Regina promised to stay in touch, and she kept that promise. Knowing she was there for him meant a great deal to Adrian.

When he returned home, Regina became part of Adrian's everyday life. She brought him meals, went with him to medical appointments, and made sure he stayed connected to the world beyond his home. She often arranged visits with old friends, making sure he stayed involved and social. It took time and effort on her part, but it made a real difference to Adrian. Over time, Adrian grew to understand Regina in a way he couldn't quite put into words, mirroring the quiet depth of her feelings for him. While in Montreal, Regina found a tailor who could custom-make shirts for Adrian. Knowing how much pride he took in his appearance, she arranged to have shirts tailored to fit him well and look smart while he was seated in his wheelchair. The attention to his wardrobe was more than practical—it reflected his personality and reminded him of who he had always been. Regina also took him to visit his mother and they would often stop by a beach on the way. He found it peaceful to sit by the ocean, watching the waves and listening to them crash on the shore. The fresh sea air mixed with the smell of wet sand and seaweed felt soothing and familiar, and they would spend hours talking. He told Regina about the time in Brigus South when a bottle washed ashore with a note inside. It was from a little girl in Sweden who had tossed it into the sea two years earlier. As a child, he imagined the bottle's long journey across the water and thought, *I'd like to travel the world like that bottle—maybe someday I will.* He enjoyed these outings very much.

Other things he didn't enjoy. One of the hardest adjustments after his accident was how differently people began to treat him. "It was like they couldn't see past the chair," he'd say. "Some folks looked at me like I was some kind of charity case, just pitying me. Others got way too protective, like I couldn't do anything for myself anymore. And then there were the ones who just didn't know what to say, so they'd act all awkward around me."

He understood, to some degree, why they acted that way, but it still bothered him. "The thing was, I was still the same person: same interests, same passion for life, but it was like they couldn't see *me* anymore. They only saw the disability. It wasn't easy."

During this particularly tough period in Adrian's life, Regina had a way of reminding him of the things he truly cared about and the unique talents he possessed, especially during moments when he doubted himself. She pushed him to keep going and to pursue the interests that brought him joy. Adrian found strength in her unwavering faith in him. While he was studying at Memorial, Regina was also there to help with practical tasks like writing papers, reviewing his course materials, and transcribing notes from his classes. This significantly reduced his workload, allowing him to focus on learning without the constant stress of falling behind.

Over time, Adrian and Regina's relationship settled into a familiar rhythm. Friends sometimes joked that they were like an old married couple. Regina was deeply committed and dreamed of a future where she might take him out of the Hoyles Home and care for him herself, creating a life together. Adrian, however, was more cautious. He understood the depth of Regina's kindness and devotion, but he also knew how demanding his care needs were and feared the weight it would place on her. He was not someone who found it easy to speak openly about his feelings, and so he often kept his worries to himself.

While Adrian was at Memorial University from 1969 to 1973, the institution was undergoing changes, mirroring the shifting dynamics of Newfoundland itself. The traditional cod fishery, once the cornerstone of the province's economy, was in decline, bringing economic uncertainty that was felt across the island, including on campus. Memorial University was expanding rapidly, introducing new programs and departments to serve a growing student body. This growth fostered a vibrant atmosphere but also gave rise to tensions, particularly as students grappled with the pressures of rising tuition and economic instability.

Amid this backdrop of change, student activism flourished. Protests and demonstrations became common, with students voicing their concerns over issues ranging from university policy to broader social and economic inequalities. Adrian, always passionate about fairness and inclusion, participated in the 1972 sit-in protest against tuition increases, reflecting his belief in accessible education and equal opportunities for all students. Years later, he reminisced about that event, recalling the protest in vivid detail. Back then, smoking was still allowed in public spaces, and Adrian, a dedicated smoker, rarely went without a cigarette. Because of his condition, someone would place the cigarette in his mouth and light it for him. He laughed as he remembered always having ash dangling precariously. During the sit-in, the administration building was packed, and the air grew thick with smoke. "You could barely see the person next to you," Adrian recounted, describing the haze that filled the room as the hours wore on.

At the Spring Convocation in 1973, Adrian rolled confidently across the stage in his wheelchair to accept his Bachelor of Arts degree from Dr. G. A. Frecker, the Chancellor of Memorial University. It was a moment of immense pride, not only for Adrian but also for everyone who had supported him along the way. Unbeknownst to many at the time, he was making history as the first quadriplegic graduate of the University. The audience erupted in applause—their cheers filled with admiration and respect for Adrian's perseverance and dedication. His accomplishment was more than an academic milestone—it was a powerful statement about breaking barriers and redefining what was possible. This historic moment wasn't just a personal victory; it also highlighted the importance of inclusivity and accessibility in higher education. Adrian's success paved the way for future students with disabilities, leaving a legacy of hope and progress that resonated far beyond the walls of Memorial University.

In four short years, Adrian had graduated with a bachelor's degree majoring in psychology. His success at Memorial University fuelled his ambition to reach even greater heights. With a passion for justice, he decided to pursue further studies in the field of law. He was eager to gain the skills and expertise needed to advocate for those who faced barriers similar to his own. Unfortunately, there was no law school in Newfoundland—the closest was Dalhousie University in Halifax. He applied and was accepted at Dalhousie, this time not telling administration that he was in a wheelchair.

FIFTEEN

Moving to Halifax

LEAVING THE FAMILIAR ENVIRONMENT OF THE Hoyles Home was a tough decision for Adrian. In his four years there, he had come to feel part of a community. His routine at the Hoyles Home was structured and dependable. His daily schedule was designed to suit his needs and preferences, with input from his care team, allowing him to stay as independent and comfortable as possible.

Adrian loved food, especially traditional Newfoundland meals. Every Friday night, a family member would bring him a special meal featuring his favourite local dishes. Jiggs dinner, meat cakes, and hearty fish dishes were often on the menu. Carmel included his special requests like turkey necks or blood pudding. Junior's wife, Sheila, would sometimes bring along a feed of cod tongues, and it would send the two brothers back in time, reminiscing about long days on the wharf in Brigus South, cutting out cod tongues and selling them for ten cents a dozen. In addition to his family's support, a neighbour from across the street often brought over home-cooked meals. The neighbour's husband, who had been at Mount Cashel with Adrian, remembered how much he enjoyed a good, hearty meal and took comfort in knowing Adrian was being well cared for.

Leaving this supportive environment was tough, but Adrian had a clear goal in mind, which kept him focused and motivated as he prepared for his move to Halifax. Travelling by air as a quadriplegic in the 1970s was quite difficult, as accessibility options were extremely limited. Boarding ramps, lifts, and specialized seating arrangements were not standard, making the process of getting onto the plane difficult. For Adrian, this would be his first time flying on a commercial airline since his accident, as previous trips between St. John's and Montreal had been arranged through air ambulances. Before his flight to Halifax, the airline was notified of Adrian's condition, and special assistance was requested.

On the day of the flight, the ground crew was involved in coordinating his boarding and providing physical assistance. They used lifting straps or carrying chairs to help transfer him into the aircraft, since no specialized equipment like ramps or lifts were available. Adrian needed someone with him on the flight to help get him into his seat, assist with things like food or drinks, and handle his personal care during the trip. Despite the challenges of flying in the 1970s, Adrian's upbeat attitude and his large circle of friends meant he was never short on help. When his companion asked how he was doing he replied, "Fine, just waiting for the circus to begin." His ability to joke about the situation made everyone around him smile, and it was clear that, no matter the difficulty, Adrian was able to roll with the punches.

Society's understanding and awareness of disabilities in the 1970s were much different than they are today, and that certainly impacted the level of accommodation and support provided by airline staff and fellow passengers. Over the years, Adrian endured several uncomfortable and sometimes painful airplane trips. On one occasion, many years later, he ended up with bruises and bumps during a flight. Aircraft weren't designed to accommodate someone of Adrian's size, which made air travel especially challenging and often led to physical discomfort and injury. Each flight highlighted the persistent accessibility challenges in transportation, an issue Adrian later addressed through his advocacy work. Despite all this, he managed to find humour in the situation, often joking that boarding an airplane felt like preparing for an extreme sport. With a grin, he'd quip that he needed a whole pit crew just to get on the plane. It turned into something he could joke about, helping to lighten the mood and make a stressful situation a bit easier.

On his way to Halifax, Adrian faced more than just the physical challenges of boarding a plane. He also had to think about starting a demanding course of study and adjusting to life in a new city, which made the journey even more complicated. The uncertainty of it all could have been overwhelming at times. Several students Adrian had met at Memorial were also starting university in Halifax, so he already had a small circle of friends. The assistance of his fellow Newfoundland students provided him with the encouragement, guidance, and friendship that he needed to navigate this new chapter in his life.

When Adrian moved to Halifax, he carefully sought out the resources and facilities he would need in his new surroundings. He reached out to professionals and support services to help him settle in and make sure his needs were addressed. This included connecting with disability support programs and local community organizations that provided assistance to people with disabilities.

When Adrian applied to Dalhousie University, he didn't mention needing a wheelchair. According to his brother-in-law, Bob McGrath, when the university learned of Adrian's situation, they told him there wasn't a chair available for him. Adrian's reply? "That's okay, I'll bring my own chair." Although Dalhousie didn't have the proper facilities for students with disabilities back then, Adrian was accepted and made up his mind to make it work. Much like his time at Memorial University, his determination and hard work helped him get through. His efforts not only allowed him to succeed but also played a part in making the university more accessible for students who came after him.

He settled on living at Pine Haven Estates, a long-term care facility. For the first two years, he had to depend on taxis to take him back and forth to university. This had been the case at the Hoyles Home as well, so he knew the drill. His daily commute to school by taxi, especially with the added complexity of his wheelchair, was no small feat. The heavy electric wheelchair had to be broken down and put in the car trunk and he had to be manoeuvred into the taxi and out again when he reached his destination. In just a few weeks, he had formed a good relationship with several taxi drivers, becoming a familiar face in their circles. Sometimes they shared local gossip or pointed out spots popular with students, giving him insight into the local area. However, one day on his way to class, Adrian was accidentally dropped, resulting in an injury that left him bedridden for three weeks. This was a tough period for him, both physically and academically, as his recovery interrupted his studies. Even though it was a setback, he regained his momentum with even more determination to succeed. By the start of his third year, Pine Haven Estates acquired an "Ironsides" van equipped with a hydraulic lift for his wheelchair. This new transportation option made getting to university much smoother and allowed him to concentrate on his studies rather than worrying about logistics.

Adrian made sure to mix some fun into his time in Halifax—it wasn't all about studying. He enjoyed going out with friends to bars and listening to live music. He especially liked following

Newfoundland bands when they were in town, and Ryan's Fancy was a favourite. He'd gotten to know them after they played the benefit concert for him, and he made it a point to see them whenever he could. One of his favourite spots was the Black Knight Lounge, a cozy place where he could always count on having a good time. Inevitably, he'd run into someone from St. John's. It seemed like everyone knew who he was, even if he didn't always know them. He'd usually shrug it off with a simple, "I'm not here that often, you know!" and carry on enjoying the evening.

While at Memorial University, Adrian became good friends with a fellow student named Paul Dicks. Like Adrian, Paul decided to study law at Dalhousie. Adrian asked Paul if he would help him with his studies and Paul gladly agreed. The Government of Newfoundland saw the need and agreed to help, giving Paul a stipend to be Adrian's tutor. Paul would share his notes and read articles and papers aloud to Adrian, whose remarkable memory allowed him to retain just about everything he heard. Adrian and Paul's friendship grew and began to extend beyond university life.

When Paul visited Adrian at Pine Haven Estates, there was always a mix of visitors around, happy to lend a hand if Adrian needed anything. His room became a gathering place for a wide group of friends and acquaintances. On Saturday nights, people gathered to watch *Hockey Night in Canada*. They placed bets, playfully teased each other about their favourite teams, and cheered or groaned with every goal. The excitement reached its peak when Adrian's beloved Canadiens, the Habs, were playing. A devoted fan since their golden era in the 1950s, Adrian often reminisced about those glory days. It was a time when the team dominated the NHL with stars like Maurice "Rocket" Richard, Jean Béliveau, and Jacques Plante. He felt the league's expansion, beginning in 1967, diluted the league's rich tradition and intense rivalries.

For Adrian, the golden years of the Habs symbolized excellence, with Stanley Cup victories seeming inevitable. Adrian's deep love for the Canadiens often made him the target of some good-natured teasing, especially when his team struggled. Friends would playfully remind him of the Habs' waning dominance, joking, "Looks like the glory days are on *rewind*, Adrian!" These Saturday nights were a treasured ritual, helping everyone unwind after a busy week.

Adrian thrived at Dalhousie. The rigorous demands of law school were no different for Adrian than for other students. As with his time at Memorial University, he welcomed the demands. He committed tomes of legal process and precedent to memory and finished courses on time. Not content to scrape by with a pass, he got good grades. Exam papers were given to him to be completed within twenty-four hours. He wrote exams through a second party, a faculty appointed legal secretary, who transcribed his dictation into a recording machine. He found this situation both humorous and interesting, often joking that his exams had a higher word count than his professors' lectures.

Each exam was dictated to a different secretary, whose identity was unknown to Adrian until his exam started. In all likelihood the law school wanted to ensure he had no advantage over his fellow students. In May 1976, he was awarded an LLB, becoming the first quadriplegic person in North America to obtain a law degree.

During Adrian's time in Halifax, he had the good fortune of working with Donald Kerr, Queen's Counsel (QC). Together they drafted and presented modern legislation affecting the disabled. Their collaborative efforts left a lasting impact as this legislation would later be the draft for many similar legislations in other provinces throughout Canada and other jurisdictions within the British Commonwealth.

Paul Dicks returned to Newfoundland after graduation and set up his law practice in Corner Brook. Elected Liberal Member of the House of Assembly in Humber West in 1989, he served as Speaker of the House and held multiple cabinet posts, including Justice, Finance, and Mines and Energy. After Dicks entered politics, he spent more time in St. John's and re-established his relationship with Adrian.

Adrian's friends were there at Dalhousie when he wheeled onto the platform to receive his degree. As he received his diploma, the room burst into thunderous applause celebrating not just his academic accomplishments but also his resilience and remarkable journey. In the front row, his mother, Maggie, and Aunt Mary beamed with pride, their eyes shining with tears. Maggie and Aunt Mary had travelled all the way from Newfoundland, and seeing Adrian reach this milestone after everything he had endured meant more to him than words could say. After the ceremony, he lingered to greet friends and family, taking a moment to let the joy of the day sink in. He even paused for a few photos, smiling for the camera despite feeling tired from the long day.

SIXTEEN

Returning to St. John's

ADRIAN ARRIVED BACK IN ST. JOHN'S AFTER three years in Halifax and returned to live at his old haunt, the Hoyles Home. He articled under the Deputy Minister of Justice, Vincent McCarthy Q.C., who subsequently became Judge McCarthy. In May of 1977, Adrian was called to the Bar and subsequently received an appointment with the Department of Justice. Adrian's admission to the Bar of Newfoundland was marked by a formal ceremony held at the Supreme Court building.

When it came time for the ceremony, Adrian's family realized the Supreme Court building wasn't wheelchair accessible. Even though it was a major obstacle, they found a way to get him inside. The experience stayed with Adrian, making him more aware of how many places weren't accessible. It strengthened his determination to work for changes that would make public spaces easier for everyone to use, no matter their physical abilities.

The new wheelchair-accessible van at the Hoyles Home brought a significant change to Adrian's mobility, giving him greater freedom. He could now travel more easily to and from the Confederation Building, allowing him to maintain a sense of independence. He became good friends with the attendants who drove the van, and these friendships became an important part of his life. Adrian liked to joke that with the new van, he had become the Hoyles Home's unofficial tour guide.

At the Confederation Building, he was provided with a telephone with just two buttons, on and off. To make a call, he'd press the on button, tell the operator the number, and they'd connect him. He had a great memory for phone numbers and became a friendly, familiar voice to the operators at Newfoundland Telephone. When he called, he often started with, "Connect me with Carmel," and the operators would put him through. Adrian enjoyed chatting with the operators, asking about their lives and where they were from. He often knew someone from their hometowns. "You must know so-and-so," he'd say, and before long, the call would shift into a ten-minute conversation about mutual acquaintances.

Adrian depended on his caregivers at the Hoyles Home for his daily needs and grew close to many of them. One of them, Chris Underhay, became very important to him. Planning trips outside the province took a lot of effort. Chris always travelled with Adrian, providing care and friendship. Chris wasn't just a caregiver to Adrian; outside of their daily routines, Chris took him on outings around St. John's, helping him pick out meaningful gifts for special occasions or just dropping into a bar for a drink. They went to sports events and parties, visited friends, and over time, Chris became like family. Their relationship wasn't one-sided, Adrian gave just as much back, offering wisdom, encouragement, and advice. They would talk for hours about all sorts of things. Adrian felt comfortable opening up about his relationship with Regina, something he didn't usually discuss. Chris would also discuss his personal life, often saying, "It's interesting how different our lives are, but in the ways that really matter, we're more alike than we think."

Adrian's graduation and his subsequent calling to the Bar attracted a great deal of attention. The story even caught the interest of the producers of *Front Page Challenge*, a popular Canadian game show on CBC where journalists would guess the news story behind a mystery guest and then interview them. Adrian was the first person from Newfoundland to appear on the show, and the headline for his appearance was "First Quadriplegic Lawyer to Earn a Law Degree." *Front Page Challenge* was a beloved legacy program in Canada, known for its long run and widespread popularity, especially in Newfoundland. After his appearance, he received an outpouring of positive feedback and recognition from across the country.

Being featured on *Front Page Challenge* brought Adrian more attention than he expected. The show reached a wide audience, helping to highlight his achievements and the challenges faced by people with physical disabilities. One person who noticed Adrian's story was Jean Chrétien, who was the Justice Minister at the time. Chrétien visited Adrian to hear first-hand about his experience. Adrian appreciated Chrétien's genuine interest, particularly his focus on accessibility issues and his openness to supporting changes that could improve the lives of people with disabilities. During their conversation, Adrian reminisced about spending time in Shawinigan, Chrétien's hometown. While working on the DEW Line in Labrador, he frequently travelled back and forth to Quebec as part of his duties. Chrétien seemed to enjoy hearing this connection. The meeting highlighted the power of advocacy and it was clear that Chrétien was not only willing to listen but also open to backing future laws that could address accessibility challenges.

Following the airing of the *Front Page Challenge* show, Adrian was approached by a prominent film production company interested in making a movie about his life. The offer was enticing, but Adrian turned it down, a decision that disappointed his niece, Jeanine. She had been thrilled at the prospect and was eager for the project to come to life. After he made the decision, Adrian and Jeanine sat down for an open and heartfelt conversation. He talked about his challenges and the realities of living as a quadriplegic, explaining how these daily struggles influenced his decision to decline the offer. He spoke candidly about the physical limitations he faced, detailing how even small tasks required significant effort and planning.

He explained that his energy levels varied from day to day, and even fun activities could sometimes leave him feeling tired or uncomfortable. He talked about his worries regarding the project and whether he could make a real impact without risking his health. As they spoke, Jeanine began to see that Adrian's hesitation wasn't about lacking motivation, but rather the need to think carefully about every decision for his well-being. Their conversation gave her a better understanding of his daily life and helped her appreciate the thoughtful decisions he had to make. This was just one of many talks they had, where Adrian shared his values, giving Jeanine insight into the decisions and sacrifices that shaped his life.

SEVENTEEN

Life at the Department of Justice

AFTER FINISHING HIS ARTICLING, ADRIAN became part of the civil division at the Department of Justice. His role primarily focused on legal matters involving non-criminal disputes and issues. His responsibilities were diverse, including offering legal advice and representation to government departments and agencies, drafting and reviewing contracts, legislation, and regulations, and providing counsel on administrative law and human rights matters. He served as legal advisor to the Departments of Wildlife, Education, Tourism, and Career Development and Advanced Studies.

In addition to his other responsibilities, Adrian was entrusted with overseeing United Nations Conventions and International Law. This role involved a broad array of tasks related to understanding, applying, and ensuring compliance with international legal standards and agreements. His duties included legal analysis, providing policy advice, coordinating between governments, monitoring compliance, and representing both domestic and international legal matters. This work helped ensure that

Newfoundland and Labrador fulfilled its international obligations and integrated these standards into its legal and policy frameworks. Adrian particularly enjoyed this aspect of his role as before his accident he had worked with the United Nations. His background in international law and agreements made him particularly well suited for this responsibility.

The Department of Justice was located on the fifth floor of the Confederation Building, and when Adrian joined, they had to develop a special evacuation plan in case of an emergency. His office was located in an alcove that jutted out from the building, making it accessible by a truck fitted with a ladder if needed. To ensure a swift response if needed, the department worked closely with the local fire department to make them aware of the specific access needs for his office. This communication helped guarantee that emergency teams would be prepared if the need arose.

The department also made efforts to accommodate Adrian's needs, offering a flexible work schedule so he could return to the Hoyles Home as needed. While his physical abilities below his neck were limited to some motion in his right hand, he used it with skill to operate both an electric wheelchair and a telephone. He had a speakerphone that he could control by pressing the number pad, and he could also turn the pages of documents with his index finger. These accommodations allowed Adrian to work independently and manage his responsibilities effectively.

Adrian's colleagues fondly recall his innovative methods for managing tasks. Using a rubber thimble on his index finger, he flipped through documents while speaking into a Dictaphone recorder. His ability to rely solely on memory to recall the contents of previous pages—since he could only move them forward—highlighted his extraordinary cognitive skills. Equally impressive was his use of a pencil held in his mouth to turn pages, demonstrating not just his resourcefulness but also his determination to make the situation work. Years later, Chief Justice Alex Hickman wrote, "I had the opportunity to work with Adrian for two years. While his disability was very challenging, the strength of his opinions reflected a sharp, well-trained mind and a strong dedication to his work."

Adrian had a great memory, like his mother, which helped him quickly recall laws, cases, and legal principles. This made him more efficient and effective in his work, and his natural ability to connect with people made them eager to support him. His ability to find humour in everyday situations created a positive atmosphere. He even started a weekly betting pool on how often the elevator would break down. The relationships he formed at work were important as he relied on the staff for much of his daily routine. He felt comfortable asking any of the secretaries to help with personal tasks, like combing his hair, wiping his brow, or adjusting his collar to make sure he always looked his best. He cared about his appearance and didn't hesitate to do whatever it took to maintain it. The staff helped without hesitation or discomfort, even though these tasks were intimate. This care was a natural extension of the camaraderie and mutual respect Adrian had built with his coworkers, and became a simple part of the daily work routine.

In the mid-1980s, Tom Mills was a young lawyer when he joined the Department of Justice. At that time, the department had a small number of senior lawyers, including Adrian, who took Tom under his wing. He became a mentor and a guiding figure, offering Tom invaluable insights into the inner workings of the department and the broader legal field. Adrian's mentorship was instrumental in helping Tom navigate the intricacies of his new role and develop his legal career.

This role of mentorship was one that Adrian particularly cherished. He relished the opportunity to shape the next generation of lawyers, ensuring they were well equipped to handle the demands of their profession. In the 1980s, a hierarchical system prevailed, with senior lawyers often looking down on newcomers. Adrian, however, was different. He welcomed the young lawyers warmly and took every chance to pass on his knowledge and insights. Adrian's personality and talent for storytelling made him an engaging teacher. He was a source of fun and positivity that brightened the workplace.

On Friday afternoons after a busy week, Adrian would join the other lawyers for a drink in the Law Library. His colleagues recall him as a highly sociable person who loved telling stories, joking around, and never missing an opportunity to have a drink and socialize. They fondly recall that after a few drinks, Adrian would often break into song, delighting everyone around him. Adrian loved to tell everyone about his time in the school choir, when he had been told to mouth the words. Once he left school, though, nothing could stop him from singing his heart out. His love of music was evident to anyone who heard him.

In the 1980s, lawyers in the Justice Department were not covered by the Public Service Act, leaving them without recourse for any employment issues that arose. Tom Mills joined Adrian on a committee that sought to establish an entity to collectively address these issues. Although this effort was unsuccessful, it was one of the many initiatives Adrian participated in as an attempt to improve working conditions for everyone.

Soon after Adrian returned home from Halifax, he met Eric Boyd, who had started the Newfoundland branch of the Canadian Paraplegic Association in 1975. The organization aimed to help people with spinal cord injuries and other physical disabilities live independently and take part in their communities. Both Adrian and Eric saw that the biggest barrier to full participation was the lack of accessibility. They knew that change would only happen by working with local organizations that understood the issues and were dedicated to making a difference. While working at the Department of Justice, Adrian began his advocacy work, becoming a dedicated member of the disability community. He focused on raising awareness about key issues such as accessibility, employment opportunities, and discrimination. By speaking out on these topics, he helped educate both the public and policymakers, advocating for policy changes to address the barriers faced by people with disabilities. His efforts emphasized improving accessibility in public spaces, transportation, and housing.

"We don't want anything you haven't got," he said, addressing non-disabled individuals. "We just want to share in the goods and services you take for granted. Services are subsidized for able-bodied people; why not for the disabled?" He believed that education was a powerful tool in breaking down both physical and attitudinal barriers between people with disabilities and the larger community. "The public needs to be educated about the needs of the disabled, and the disabled need to be educated so they can take their place in the community as professionals and reach their full potential."

EIGHTEEN

A Special Mentor

ADRIAN BECAME A MENTOR TO MANY PEOPLE throughout his life, and he was also influenced by a mentor of his own—Don Curran of the Canadian Paraplegic Association. Curran was born in Nova Scotia; he served as a fighting officer in the RCAF during World War II, and became paralyzed from the waist down after a plane crash on takeoff for North Africa in November 1943. Don became an outstanding inspiration to all those whose lives he touched. He graduated from Dalhousie Law school in 1950 and was admitted to the bar of Nova Scotia the following year. Rather than pursuing a career as a practising lawyer, he founded the Maritime Division of the Canadian Paraplegic Association (CPA) and served as its executive director until 1984.

Don Curran dedicated himself to identifying and connecting with every individual in the Atlantic region who had suffered a spinal cord injury and, naturally, he became aware of Adrian. During Adrian's rehabilitation in Montreal, he was introduced to Don Curran. This encounter planted the seeds for Adrian's future career, though it took him a few years to realize that his decision to pursue law was significantly inspired by Don. Don's guidance and support played a crucial role in shaping Adrian's aspirations and ultimately led him down the path of legal studies.

Upon Adrian's graduation from Dalhousie, Curran, in his capacity with CPA, commented, "Adrian Battcock represents the realization of every hope the association invested in him. He is like a breath of fresh air to everyone, carrying the needs, sorrows, and worries of every Maritime paraplegic. He enhanced and inspired the lives of so many people. We expect great things from him in Newfoundland."

While Don's injury left him paraplegic and requiring the use of a wheelchair for mobility, he considered himself fortunate to retain the use of his upper body. This allowed him to maintain a degree of independence, living in his own home and managing daily tasks with relative ease. On the other hand, Adrian's injury was far more severe, rendering him quadriplegic. He required extensive personal care and medical support. His complex needs made independent living impossible at the time. Don deeply admired Adrian's resilience—the discipline, patience, and emotional strength required to live fully and lead effectively under such profound physical constraints. As Adrian began his advocacy work in Newfoundland, he frequently looked to Don for guidance. As they shared legal training, they spoke the same practical language. They talked about constitutions and bylaws, proper record keeping, clear mandates, and the importance of presenting well-prepared briefs to government officials. Don encouraged Adrian to approach advocacy the way a lawyer approaches a case: know the facts and understand the legislation.

Having Don's counsel during those formative years gave Adrian confidence and direction. It reinforced his conviction that strong provincial branches of the CPA, collaborating across Atlantic Canada, could influence public policy and bring about meaningful improvements in the lives of persons with disabilities.

NINETEEN

Disability Rights Movement

IN NEWFOUNDLAND AND LABRADOR, A SMALL BUT dedicated group of individuals became leaders in the disability rights movement. These passionate activists not only supported local efforts but also took active roles on the national stage, pushing the cause forward within the province and across Canada. Their work helped ensure the needs and perspectives of persons with disabilities were included in broader discussions, strengthening the national disability rights movement.

Adrian was one of these tireless advocates who worked throughout the 1970s and 1980s on various initiatives. He was committed to improving accessibility, inclusivity, and the rights of people with disabilities during a critical time of social change and policy reform. He collaborated with other advocates, community groups, and policymakers to push for legislative changes, raise awareness, and make sure marginalized voices were heard. His efforts were key in driving change and establishing more inclusive societal norms.

Adrian's particular focus was on improving accessibility in transportation, housing, and employment for people with disabilities. Working within the government, he used his position to influence both new laws and existing policies, making practical changes to create a more accessible society. His unique role allowed him to make significant strides in improving life for people with disabilities, something he understood from his own lived experience.

The Disability Rights Movement in North America emerged due to the increasing disparities between disabled veterans and civilians with disabilities that became more pronounced in the aftermath of World War II. Civilian people with disabilities as well as those within the veterans' movement advocated for the expansion of services to all who needed them regardless of the cause of one's disability. Activists contended that disabled individuals deserved the same opportunities as everyone else to engage fully in society. They insisted that this meant not only being able to move through public spaces and access public services but also having the necessary support systems to live autonomously and find meaningful employment.

This push for equal access encompassed everything from physical accommodations, like wheelchair ramps and accessible public transportation, to more abstract supports such as policies that promoted employment opportunities and protected against discrimination. By the 1970s, people with disabilities started forming their own groups to advocate for equal rights. Activists struggled to establish a disability rights movement led by persons with disabilities rather than by sympathetic parents and professionals. This shift empowered disabled individuals to voice their own needs, fostering a more authentic and representative movement.

On December 9, 1975, the United Nations issued the *Declaration on the Rights of Disabled Persons*. The declaration outlined key rights for disabled people and encouraged member countries to enact legislation and promote initiatives to safeguard these rights and opportunities. The declaration was hailed by growing numbers of disability rights activists, who advocated for new legal rights to support the advancement and protection of disabled persons in all areas of civic life, including economic security and self-reliance.

The UN International Year for Disabled Persons (IYDP), celebrated in 1981, represented a high mark in the pursuit of disability rights in Canada. The IYDP and the subsequent UN Decade of Disabled Persons (1983–92) fostered an unprecedented level of public and political interest in Canada regarding the rights and opportunities afforded to people with disabilities. This increased general awareness of disability issues fuelled campaigns to include disability in the *Charter of Rights and Freedoms*. Initially denied on the suspicion that the term "disability" was too vague and open to interpretation, intensive efforts eventually ensured its inclusion as a protected category in the final draft of the *Charter*.

With the proclamation of the IYDP in 1981, came a significant amount of federal money aimed at determining what services were available and identifying areas where gaps existed, among other objectives. In Newfoundland, three students were hired to conduct a survey of laws impacting persons with disabilities. This project was funded by the Government of Canada and delivered through the Newfoundland Legal Aid Commission, which contributed resources, management, and additional support. Adrian served as the mentor on the disability rights component of the initiative.

One of the students, Anne Marie Rose, was excited about the project and eager to meet Adrian, having heard so much about him from her mother. Her mother, Rosemary Rose, had worked as a secretary in the Political Science department at Memorial University when Adrian was a student. She spoke very fondly of him, recalling his popularity with all the faculty in the department and remembering how she used to transcribe notes for him. Rosemary often shared stories about Adrian's charisma, which made a lasting impression on Anne Marie. When Anne Marie finally told Adrian who her mother was, he was delighted and launched straight into stories about Rosemary, laughing as he said that without her careful notetaking, he might never have passed half his courses.

Anne Marie described Adrian as a big-picture person who guided them through every aspect of the process. He emphasized that it was essential their work fit into the broader context of society. Anne Marie remarked how Adrian could quote, chapter and verse, any statute or law. A few years later, Anne Marie joined the Department of Justice as a solicitor. In this capacity she found Adrian to be very supportive of his colleagues, always encouraging them to strive for their best and pursue their goals with passion.

Under Adrian's expert guidance, the students created a pivotal document titled "Rights of the Disabled and Survey of the Law in Newfoundland and Labrador," which was published in 1982. This comprehensive report meticulously examined the existing legal framework and highlighted the rights and needs of individuals with disabilities within the province. The document received widespread acclaim for its thorough analysis and practical recommendations, earning a reputation as one of the best of its kind in the country. It set a high standard and served as a model for other jurisdictions looking to enhance their own disability rights legislation and policies. Adrian's mentorship helped the students gain a solid understanding of disability law, making it easier for them to grasp both its shortcomings and practical applications. He enjoyed working with the students, finding their energy and passion inspiring, and was quite proud of the document they produced. Their enthusiasm reminded him of his own early days heading off to work on the DEW Line, when he first experienced the independence and pride that came with responsibility.

TWENTY

Community Services Council

DURING THIS PERIOD, ADRIAN ALSO BECAME deeply involved with the Community Services Council (CSC).

The establishment of the CSC in St. John's emerged from a broader push for community-based solutions to social issues during the 1970s. This organization was born out of a desire to address gaps in communication and coordination among various social service organizations. The CSC sought to foster collaboration between government, non-profits, and community groups to improve the delivery of social services. It aimed to empower local communities by facilitating partnerships and sharing resources. It provided training to strengthen organizations working in areas such as poverty reduction, health, and housing. Over time, the CSC became a central hub for social planning and advocacy in Newfoundland and Labrador, helping to shape policies and practices that enhanced community well-being.

In its first decade, the organization focused on addressing the fragmentation among social service groups, particularly those providing services to persons with disabilities. The Physically Handicapped Service Centre (HUB) and the Newfoundland branch of the Canadian Paraplegic Association (CPA) had recently been established, joining a number of other organizations serving individuals with disabilities. The CSC played a pivotal role in bringing these diverse organizations and concerned individuals together, encouraging a collaborative approach to tackle issues facing the disabled community. By uniting these groups, the CSC helped create a more cohesive and effective network, improving the overall quality and impact of services offered to those in need.

In the early 1980s, the CSC took on the critical issue of housing by establishing the Community Housing and Support Services Committee, where Adrian played an active role. This committee focused on creating purpose-built housing that addressed the changing needs of the community, with a particular emphasis on accessible living spaces. Over the course of eight or nine years, the committee successfully oversaw the construction of several housing cooperatives, ensuring that these developments included units designed to be fully accessible and inclusive.

The 1980s marked a significant period of deinstitutionalization, during which individuals with disabilities were transitioned from large institutional settings into community-based living arrangements. This shift aimed to promote greater autonomy, dignity, and integration for people with disabilities, recognizing their right to live independently and participate fully in society. It involved reallocating resources to support community-based services and fostering environments where individuals could receive tailored care and support while enjoying greater social inclusion.

This process of deinstitutionalization spanned many years and required the concerted efforts of numerous organizations, advocates, and policymakers. It involved a fundamental shift in attitudes towards individuals with disabilities, moving away from the previous model of isolating them in large institutions towards one that emphasized community integration and support. Advocates played a crucial role in pushing for policy changes that prioritized individual rights and autonomy. They worked tirelessly to raise awareness about the potential of people with disabilities to thrive in community settings with appropriate support. This advocacy spurred legislative reforms and funding initiatives aimed at expanding community-based services such as supportive housing, vocational training, and health-care access.

Changing societal attitudes were integral to the success of deinstitutionalization. There was a growing recognition that segregating people with disabilities deprived them of their dignity and limited their opportunities for personal growth and social interaction. As perceptions evolved, so did public policy, resulting in a gradual dismantling of large institutions and the establishment of more inclusive and person-centred care models. Overall, the process of deinstitutionalization was a complex and multifaceted endeavour that involved collaborative efforts across various sectors. It underscored a commitment to human rights and social justice, aiming to create a more equitable and inclusive society.

The challenges faced by the disability community were numerous and wide ranging, but it became apparent that without addressing the issue of housing, and by extension, the accessibility of buildings, progress in other areas would not be possible. In 1977, the CSC established the Building Accessibility Committee, which took on the critical task of improving accessibility in buildings for people with disabilities. Over the next four years, the committee conducted extensive research and analysis to understand the specific barriers that existed in public and private buildings.

Their efforts involved collaboration with a wide range of professionals, including architects, engineers, and property owners, as well as government officials and community representatives. By engaging experts and stakeholders from various sectors, the committee worked to develop practical solutions and advocate for changes in building design, ensuring that accessibility became a key consideration in both new constructions and renovations. This initiative laid the groundwork for more inclusive infrastructure across the province.

Adrian's role at the CSC required careful management of his time and energy, as he balanced his volunteer responsibilities with his position as a government employee. In practical terms, this meant reviewing policy documents, drafting briefs, and preparing recommendations as the Justice Department worked on the Building Accessibility Act legislation. By staying organized, disciplined, and focused, Adrian was able to contribute effectively both as a government employee and as a volunteer with the Building Accessibility Committee. Outside of his professional and volunteer commitments, he maintained a full and active personal life. The 1980s were a time of mischief, fun, and bold adventures for Adrian—proving that a wheelchair wasn't going to keep him from living life to the fullest. He had a playful streak and one of his favourite pastimes was good-naturedly tormenting friends and colleagues—fully aware that being in a wheelchair gave him a unique edge. "What are they going to do, chase me?" he'd joke with a wicked grin. He delighted in catching people off guard, knowing that most were too polite to retaliate. He fully embraced the fact that most people weren't sure how to respond when he pushed boundaries. "Nobody's going to yell at the guy in the wheelchair," he'd say with a chuckle. And if anyone did? He'd play innocent, rolling his eyes and saying, "What? Just trying to lighten the mood!"

Adrian spent many nights at the Strand Lounge at the Avalon Mall, especially when Ryan's Fancy were performing. He had a standing arrangement with the staff, who always made sure he had the best seat in the house (his own), front and centre, with a perfect view of the stage. He loved nothing more than the mix of jigs, reels, and ballads. With a little encouragement and perhaps a drink or two, he'd sing along. He could always persuade friends to take him out, and once they were out, he was a master at convincing them to stay for just one more drink. Ryan's Fancy held a special place in Adrian's heart. He never forgot their participation in the 1969 benefit concert that came before his university days, their generosity, and the confidence it gave him at a time when his future felt uncertain. Looking back on that time, he couldn't help but marvel on how far he had come.

Weekends were for laughter, stories, and friendship, but Monday mornings always meant a return to the work that gave his life such strong purpose.

TWENTY-ONE

The Building Accessibility Act

WORKING WITHIN THE DEPARTMENT OF JUSTICE, Adrian and his colleagues played a central role in drafting the Building Accessibility Act, developing the legal framework that would guide accessibility standards in the province. The Act was introduced in the House of Assembly in 1981. As the first legislation of its kind in Canada, it represented a major step forward for Newfoundland and its commitment to inclusion. This landmark legislation marked a crucial step forward in ensuring accessible environments for all citizens. The purpose of the Act was to provide people with physical and sensory disabilities access to public buildings, apartment-type buildings, hotels and building links, and to ensure compliance with buildings accessibility standards. Additionally, the Building Accessibility Act established mechanisms for enforcement and compliance.

The passing of the Act had major benefits for persons with disabilities as it ensured equal access to public spaces, helped with navigating the environment more easily, and fostered a greater sense of autonomy and self-sufficiency. Furthermore, it opened up businesses and services to a wider customer base, facilitated the participation of persons with disabilities in social, cultural, and recreational activities, and educated the public and private sectors on the importance of accessibility. The Building Accessibility Act indeed represented a pivotal moment in advocating for a more inclusive society. While its passage was a crucial first step, the subsequent phases of implementation were marked by extensive collaboration and consultation, including the involvement of the Coordinating Support Committee and the Provincial Government. Together, they worked closely with various community groups to address the feasibility of the Act and assess what aspects might have been overlooked during its initial drafting.

This legislation was supported by an advisory board, which played a crucial role in guiding its development and ensuring its relevance to the needs of the community. Additionally, it incorporated an appeals mechanism to provide a fair and structured process for individuals to challenge decisions or seek reconsideration. Adrian served on the Appeals Tribunal. If an individual or company felt wronged by a board decision, they had the right to submit a written appeal within a determined time frame. The Tribunal would meet periodically to review and make a determination on any appeals. Their decisions were crucial in ensuring fairness and adherence to the established regulations.

The CSC continued to play a key role during this time. Nonprofit organizations recognized that if they were advocating for accessibility in public buildings, they needed to make sure their own spaces were accessible too. Many of these groups were working out of older buildings, so they started efforts to ensure their facilities met accessibility standards. This often meant moving to rental spaces that could be easily updated, adding ramps to entrances, installing elevators when possible, widening doorways, and redesigning restrooms to accommodate people with disabilities.

The impact of the Act extended well beyond its passage. Its success depended on continuous oversight to ensure that public spaces met the new accessibility standards and on ongoing efforts to build public support. Changing attitudes toward accessibility was a slow but essential process, requiring education to emphasize the importance of inclusivity. Despite these challenges, the Act laid the groundwork for future generations to benefit. Its vision of a barrier-free society stands as a testament to the persistence and collective effort that followed its introduction. Adrian's role was to closely follow the progress of the work and make sure that existing buildings were updated to meet the accessibility standards.

Enforcing the Act required constant vigilance, supported by a committed group of volunteers. However, despite their hard work, issues continued to arise. For example, in one case, an elevator was installed in a building, but the key to operate it was only accessible on the second floor, making the elevator practically useless for those who needed it. This situation illustrates the ongoing struggle to fully achieve the goals of the Building Accessibility Act. Even today, ensuring accessibility is a continuous challenge, requiring ongoing commitment and attention to address and correct such oversights.

Throughout the 1980s, Adrian played an active role on the Board of Directors for several non-profit organizations, gaining invaluable first-hand experience and influence in efforts to improve accessibility in public and private buildings. His positions on these boards allowed him to be directly involved in decision-making processes and to advocate for the importance of meeting strict accessibility standards. His insight into the issues faced by individuals with disabilities was essential in shaping the direction of these initiatives, ensuring that renovations and new constructions were designed with inclusivity in mind. As a board member, Adrian was not only able to push for policies that prioritized accessibility, he also had the opportunity to monitor and guide the actual implementation of these changes. This helped ensure these organizations were not just meeting legal requirements, but also setting a higher standard for accessibility that went beyond the minimum.

In recognition of his achievements and work for the disabled, Adrian received the C. A. Pippy Award for handicapped person of the year in 1981. The following year, April 1982, Adrian was invited to attend the Achievers' Dinner hosted by Her Majesty the Queen in Ottawa at the time of the signing of the constitution. When Adrian was presented to Queen Elizabeth, Governor General Ed Schreyer acknowledged his advocacy efforts praising his dedication to the cause of accessibility.

Adrian loved nothing more than sharing special occasions with family. He enjoyed hosting and attending gatherings for birthdays, holidays, or other milestones. He could be impulsive and outrageous, but he was always generous. It wasn't unusual for him to book a table at the Hotel St. John's or Papa's Restaurant in Churchill Square for the family. When asked, "how many?" He'd reply, "a table for six—I'll bring my own chair." Sometimes, with very little notice, he would call Junior, Carmel, or Sheila and have them pick up his mother and head to the restaurant. There would be no conversation. "I have a table booked at Papa's, bring Mom and I'll see you there at six." These two restaurants were favourites of Adrian's, and the staff at both places would go out of their way to accommodate him. They knew his quirks, remembered his usual orders, and often had a sly grin ready when he walked in, as if to say, "Here comes Adrian—let the fun begin." Meals with him were never just dinner; they were lively, full of laughter, and sometimes a little mischief. The dinners may have ended, but Adrian's work to open doors—for everyone—continued.

TWENTY-TWO

The Independent Living Resource Centre

ONE OF THE PIONEERING PROJECTS OF THE CSC was at first called Escasoni Place, an innovative initiative created to provide specialized care and support. The project was intended as a transitional housing solution for people who had previously lived in institutions or with family members. It offered a supportive environment where residents could develop the necessary skills for independent living, marking a significant shift towards promoting autonomy and self-sufficiency within the community. Initially, this group home accommodated six individuals, offering them a temporary residence as part of their transitional journey toward independent living. This comprehensive program attempted to address the unique needs of each resident, fostering an environment where they could gain confidence and self-sufficiency.

This initiative was deeply rooted in the broader national independent living movement and eventually evolved into the Independent Living Resource Centre. It marked a pivotal shift from simply providing housing for a small number of individuals with disabilities, to creating an organization dedicated to empowering a much larger population. The Centre became a hub for advocacy, support, and education, enabling people with disabilities to make independent decisions about their living arrangements and other aspects of their lives. This transformation highlighted a growing dedication to autonomy, personal choice, and the recognition that these principles are fundamental to improving the quality of life for individuals with disabilities.

Central to the program was the identification of key elements necessary for independent living: supportive housing, accessible transportation, home care, and supportive employment. By addressing these essential needs, the initiative aimed to break down barriers and foster an environment where people with disabilities could thrive. Building on these efforts, the initiative further evolved into the Association for Community Living. Each area—supportive housing, accessible transportation, home care, and supportive employment—required persistent advocacy, innovative problem solving, and unwavering dedication. The Association took on these complexities with a holistic approach, engaging in policy development, community outreach, and collaboration with like-minded organizations to provide comprehensive support for individuals with disabilities.

Throughout the 1980s, advocacy groups focused on supportive housing working in close partnership, addressing shared challenges, and frequently uniting around key issues. A notable routine was their weekly gathering at the Holiday Inn, fondly called the Friday Delegation. Here, they convened to share updates on their work, discuss challenges, and strategize collectively. Together, they drafted policy briefs, coordinated advocacy efforts, and made joint presentations to government bodies and other agencies.

Adrian's involvement was particularly significant because of his unique status within the movement. As both a consumer and an outspoken advocate, he brought a rare and valuable perspective to the table. His personal experience gave him insight into the real needs of the community, while his unwavering vision for change earned him widespread respect and admiration. His ability to bridge these roles made him a key figure in pushing the movement forward, ensuring that the voices of those most affected were heard. Once again, he considered moving out of the Hoyles Home and into this new facility, thinking about the greater independence it might offer. However, after giving it careful thought, he ultimately decided against it, choosing instead to remain where he was comfortable and well established.

Adrian was committed to ensuring that everyone, regardless of their circumstances, had access to adequate housing and support. He was determined not to be defined by his disability. He wanted to be recognized for his contributions, his leadership, and his vision, rather than solely as someone with a disability. His disability was just one aspect of who he was, not the central feature of his contributions or legacy.

Building on its foundational work, the CSC remained a driving force in addressing a wide range of social challenges, with a strong focus on supportive housing, community development, and advocating for marginalized groups. The CSC played a key role in bringing together government agencies, non-profit organizations, and local community members to work towards practical solutions meeting the needs of vulnerable populations. By encouraging collaboration and open dialogue, the CSC helped to create partnerships that led to meaningful change. Their efforts went beyond just identifying problems; they actively shaped policies, designed impactful programs, and ensured these initiatives were grounded in the realities faced by the people they aimed to support.

During this particularly demanding period in Adrian's life, he made a conscious effort to keep his weekends free for social activity. He had always been a student of learning, curious and full of seemingly endless stores of knowledge. He had a love for trivia and took great delight in surprising people with the most obscure and unexpected facts. When the game *Trivial Pursuit* was released and quickly became popular, it was perfectly suited to him. Adrian loved gathering a group in his room to play, and the game nights soon became lively social occasions filled with friendly competition. It often made him think back to his school days, when nearly every subject placed before him sparked his curiosity. That same curiosity never left him. Years later, it continued to shape the way he saw the world—always interested and always learning.

TWENTY-THREE

Wheelchair Accessible Bus Service and The HUB

IN 1980, ADRIAN WAS APPOINTED TO TERRA TRANSport's Management Advisory Board. Terra Transport was set up to organize CN's (the Canadian National Railway Company) operations in Newfoundland. With the opening of the Trans-Canada Highway in the province, there was a significant reduction in railway use, leading to the gradual phasing out of the railway system. In response, the Advisory Board implemented and oversaw the successful introduction of a provincial bus service with wheelchair accessibility.

This appointment was bittersweet; while Adrian recognized the significance of his role on the Advisory Committee, he couldn't help but feel deeply disappointed by the decision to end rail service. Growing up in Newfoundland, he saw first-hand how the railway had connected communities. In the 1950s, Adrian had travelled across Newfoundland a number of times by rail. He knew the impact this would have on towns that depended on the railway and felt it was a loss to the province's heritage. In later years, he often reflected on those journeys with a sense of nostalgia, recognizing the railway as a lifeline that fostered a sense of unity and opportunity for isolated communities. As he said many times, "The railway wasn't just tracks and trains; it was the glue that held these little towns together."

Adrian's appointment represented a meaningful step forward in promoting inclusivity and progress in transportation infrastructure. The introduction of a wheelchair-accessible bus service improved mobility options for individuals with disabilities, providing them with reliable and accessible transportation across the province. This initiative addressed a need for accessibility while setting a high standard for other regions. The system became a model in Canada and the United States, demonstrating how inclusive public transportation can greatly enhance independence and mobility for people with disabilities.

The same year, Adrian became the chair of the Board of Directors of The HUB (Physically Handicapped Service Centre) bringing dynamic leadership to the thriving centre. The HUB had opened its doors in 1975 in the former St. George's School on Merrymeeting Road, St. John's. A group of passionate volunteers transformed the neglected building into a vibrant service centre dedicated to supporting individuals with physical disabilities. The facility quickly became a trailblazer in fostering inclusivity and empowerment. It established the Information Centre, which was groundbreaking for its time, serving as a comprehensive resource hub for individuals with physical disabilities, their families, and professionals. The Centre housed a wide range of materials, including magazines, videos, books, and presentations, making it an invaluable tool for those seeking guidance in rehabilitation and advocacy.

Under Adrian's guidance, The HUB experienced remarkable growth, expanding its services and solidifying its role as a vital community resource. The HUB took an innovative approach to empowering individuals with disabilities. Its philosophy was to create opportunities for meaningful work and community engagement, demonstrating that people with disabilities could contribute fully in the workplace. To that end, several businesses were launched within the facility, including wheelchair, appliance, and bicycle-repair services, as well as a print shop and a trophy shop. Whenever possible, these businesses employed individuals with disabilities, providing training, skill development, and a sense of independence, while also fostering an inclusive environment where all contributions were valued.

An advisory board was established to guide entrepreneurs and train staff, fostering a comprehensive support system that encouraged entrepreneurship. While many of these ventures have since ceased operations, the print shop remains active to this day. The HUB's welcoming spaces encouraged members to share experiences, support one another, and build a sense of belonging. This blend of practical resources and personal connection transformed The HUB into a cornerstone of advocacy and empowerment, garnering recognition across North America.

As membership in The HUB increased, so did the demand for transportation services for its users. To meet this need, The HUB acquired its first van, the Handicab, and later added a second van as a backup. This initiative marked the inception of St. John's first transportation system for individuals with disabilities. Volunteer drivers were enlisted to help offset operational costs. However, despite these efforts, the system ultimately proved to be ineffective and inefficient. The HUB struggled to run the service and in 1980 representatives presented a brief to City Council asking the city to replace it with a more comprehensive plan. Starting in 1981, the provincial and municipal governments committed to covering the operating costs of transportation for persons with disabilities. Today, the City of St. John's, the City of Mount Pearl, and the Province of Newfoundland and Labrador provide a bus service for people with disabilities within the municipalities of St. John's and Mount Pearl.

As chair of The HUB, Adrian grew the organization's programs and ensured more people with disabilities had access to job opportunities. He used his position to highlight the skills and potential of disabled people, working to change outdated perceptions and encourage more inclusive workplaces. Chairing The HUB while working as a solicitor within the Department of Justice allowed Adrian to be deeply involved in the strategic and practical aspects of disability rights work in the province. He was at the forefront of grassroots advocacy, listening to the concerns of the disabled community. In his role as a solicitor, he applied his legal expertise to navigate the complexities of policy and legislation. By bridging advocacy and law, Adrian helped shape legislation that was both practical and legally sound, making a real difference in the daily lives of people with disabilities.

During Adrian's time on The HUB board, he became friendly with a young man named Paul, who had been injured in a workplace accident and was left with a spinal cord injury. Before the accident, Paul had worked in construction. He had always been active and independent, and after the injury he found it hard to adjust. When he first came to The HUB, he felt discouraged and believed no employer would take him seriously. Adrian took the time to sit and talk with him. Instead of focusing on what Paul could no longer do, he asked about his past work, his skills, and what he had enjoyed about construction. He treated Paul as someone with experience and ability. Later, Paul said it was one of the first times since his injury that he felt someone saw him as capable rather than helpless. Paul went on to find steady work and stayed in touch with Adrian over the years.

TWENTY-FOUR

Coalition of Persons with Disabilities (COD)

IN 1983, THE COALITION OF PERSONS WITH DISabilities (COD) was established as a provincial organization representing individuals with all types of disabilities. Its mission was to educate and advise community leaders and advocate for an inclusive and fair society for all people with disabilities in Newfoundland and Labrador. In 1987, as chair of the Board, Adrian prepared and released a detailed report titled *Transportation and Persons with Disabilities in the St. John's Area*. The report thoroughly examined the state of transportation services for individuals with disabilities, providing a historical overview and addressing current needs. It analyzed the demographics of those requiring accessible transportation, highlighted the community's moral and practical responsibility to provide these services, and outlined the role of government in setting regulations and fulfilling obligations. Adrian also included examples from other provinces to offer perspective and guidance. The report presented clear recommendations to improve transportation for persons with disabilities in St. John's. These recommendations included upgrading infrastructure to ensure accessibility, creating inclusive policies, and providing specialized training for transportation staff to better meet the needs of passengers. Additionally, the report stressed the importance of monitoring progress to ensure accountability and ongoing improvements.

A key focus of the report was the importance of collaboration. It emphasized the need for government agencies, advocacy groups, and individuals with disabilities to join forces in creating a transportation system that was both inclusive and efficient. The goal was to improve mobility, promote independence, and enhance the overall quality of life for people with disabilities in the region. Although the involvement of provincial and municipal government representatives in creating the report was a positive sign, Adrian knew that just recognizing the issue wouldn't lead to real change. He understood that making lasting improvements required more than just good intentions—it needed constant effort and pressure. He stayed proactive, holding government officials accountable for their promises. Through meetings, letters, and public advocacy, Adrian made sure the report didn't just sit on a shelf but led to actual improvements in transportation for people with disabilities. His tireless efforts highlighted that real change doesn't happen by just acknowledging a problem—it requires prompt, strong action to make a difference.

While the City of St. John's maintained a transportation service for persons with disabilities, it was quite limited. Through the Accessibility Action Committee, Adrian made several presentations urging the city to extend the service to include after hours and weekends. He took strong exception to a response from the city clerk's office, which stated, "Council is not responsible for the transportation services for the physically disabled, and further, due to budgetary constraints, Council would not be able to commit expenditures." In rebuttal, Adrian suggested that the city was potentially violating the Canadian Charter of Rights and Freedoms.

Adrian's advocacy stemmed from his firm belief that accessible transportation is not a luxury but a fundamental right, essential for individuals with disabilities to live independently and fully engage in society. The existing service's restrictions often left people stranded during evenings and weekends, cutting them off from work opportunities, social engagements, and vital activities. To strengthen his argument, Adrian presented testimonies from those directly impacted by the limited service, aiming to humanize the issue and sway council members through personal stories.

Adrian brought two people with him to tell their stories. First was Sandra, who lived on Waterford Bridge Road and used a wheelchair after having polio as a child. She lived on her own and had a job, but everyday life took a lot of effort and planning. She had been invited to a birthday dinner at a restaurant downtown and started calling for a cab early that afternoon. After several calls, she finally booked one for six o'clock. When the taxi arrived, it was a regular car. There was no ramp or lift. With the help of the driver, she tried to get into the seat and fit the wheelchair into the trunk, but no matter what they tried, it wouldn't fit. After about twenty minutes of trying, they gave up. Sandra went back into her apartment and missed the dinner. There was simply no way for her to get there.

The second story came from Tom. On a Saturday afternoon, Tom realized he was out of basic groceries. He lived alone in the west end of St. John's and used a wheelchair. He began calling taxi companies. The first two said they had no vehicles that could take a wheelchair. The third asked if he could transfer into a regular car. Tom could, but only with help, and it was never easy. After some effort, he managed to get to the grocery store. When he finished shopping, he phoned for a return cab and waited outside with his bags. Twenty minutes passed. Then thirty. There was no sign of the taxi. Finally, he had to go back inside and ask someone to call the company again for him. When they reached the dispatcher, he was told no driver was immediately available. Tom went back outside to wait, unsure how much longer it would take or how he would manage if the cab did not come.

The city's repeated reference to budgetary constraints only made Adrian more determined. He argued that financial limitations could not justify denying basic rights and that the city's inaction constituted discrimination under the equality provisions of the Charter. Adrian's interpretation emphasized that prioritizing inclusivity and accessibility was not only the correct ethical choice, it was also legally mandated. The back-and-forth with the city spanned several years, involving meetings, public forums, and media coverage. Adrian's persistence kept the issue in the public spotlight, rallying support from community members and advocacy groups. Though the council resisted initially, his tireless efforts gradually influenced public opinion and increased pressure on city leaders to revisit their stance. Over the years, Adrian's unwavering dedication to the cause helped to initiate small but meaningful upgrades to the service. While the broader vision of a fully accessible and extended transportation system remained unrealized for some time, his efforts laid the foundation for future change. At the same time, his personal life was shaped by these limitations, as even simple outings required careful planning and, at times, the help of others.

On April 11, 1984, in recognition of his considerable efforts and achievements, Adrian was awarded the Order of Canada, the highest civilian level of distinction in the Canadian honours system. Part of the citation read, "An accident at the hydroelectric project in Newfoundland left him a quadriplegic. Yet his example has inspired many disabled people to build successful lives." The ceremony was held at Rideau Hall in Ottawa with Adrian's mother, Maggie, his sister Carmel, and his constant travel companion, Chris Underhay, in attendance. The ceremony was a formal occasion, attended by government officials, dignitaries, and other recipients of the award. The award was conferred by the Right Honourable Jeanne Sauve, Governor General of Canada.

Getting Adrian to Ottawa for the event took a lot of effort. From arranging transportation and accommodations to making sure Rideau Hall was fully accessible, every detail was carefully planned. Family and friends gathered to celebrate before and after the ceremony, sharing their excitement and pride in Adrian's accomplishment. During the party, someone handed Adrian a drink, and with a grin, he joked, "Guess I'll need a designated driver tonight!" Soon everyone was laughing about being his designated driver. It was a true team effort, ensuring everything was in place so Adrian could enjoy the day without a hitch.

Adrian's nephew, Gerard, shared a funny story about Maggie and Carmel arriving in Ottawa. When they got into a taxi and asked the driver to take them to Rideau Hall, he seemed unsure that he should bring them to that address and suggested dropping them off somewhere else instead. Maggie and Carmel tried to convince him, but he didn't budge until Maggie pulled an official invitation out of her purse. That finally did the trick, and the driver took them to Rideau Hall. Afterwards, they joked about whether they'd need to start carrying invitations everywhere, just to prove they were serious about their destinations! Carmel and Maggie decided to make the most of their trip by visiting a few places and catching up with family. After seeing Adrian and Chris off at the airport, they made plans to visit Maggie's brother Mickey in New York. Mickey had lived in the city for 50 years, building a life there with his wife and raising their family. Over the years, he'd only made it home a handful of times, so this visit was a rare chance for them to reconnect.

Mickey was thrilled to welcome them and introduced his two sons, who immediately made their Newfoundland relatives feel at home. The family spent their time exploring New York together, visiting landmarks like the Empire State Building and taking a walk through Central Park. Maggie, ever proud of her family, brought along photos of her grandchildren and shared stories about them. She also gave Mickey all the latest updates on their hometown—everything from the new families who'd moved in, to the small shop that had recently opened. Mickey's memory of home hadn't faded a bit. He reminisced about the neighbours and families from years ago, asking about each one. Mickey realized he needed to visit and made plans to do so—he wanted his children to see the place where their father had grown up and hear the stories of his childhood.

On April 11, 1984, at Rideau Hall in Ottawa, Adrian Battcock is invested as an Officer of the Order of Canada, one of the nation's highest civilian honours. The insignia was presented by Governor General Edward Schreyer. Also pictured are Mrs. Lillian Schreyer and Esmond Butler, Secretary to the Governor General. Standing to Adrian's right are his orderly, Chris Underhay, his mother, Margaret (Maggie) Battcock, and his sister, Carmel Buckingham.

"Q" RADIO CITIZEN OF THE WEEK

ST. JOHN'S LAWYER ADRIAN BATTCOCK

Adrian Battcock, a St. John's lawyer is this weeks CJYQ Citizen Of The Week. Mr. Battcock was nominated for the determination and courage he had shown and in fact still shows in coping with life and winning despite great odds. This week's "Q" Radio Award went to a man who is a quadrapledgic and has been for the past eleven years or more, but who in spite of that handicap he did not throw in the sponge, but took the bit in his teeth and created a new life for himself. He enrolled at Memorial University where he received his B.A., then it was on to Delhousie University Law School, then a year of articling with the justice department, then came the objective he had worked and struggled so hard for, being called to the bar of Newfoundland, as a full fledged Lawyer, last may. A great accomplishment under the hardest of circumstances, accomplished by a man among men, the CJYQ Citizen of the Week, Mr. Adrian Battcock of St. John's.

He's going to meet the Queen

Adrian Battcock, a lawyer with the provincial justice department, will be in Ottawa Saturday to meet with Queen Elizabeth II and witness the signing of the Canadian Constitution. Battcock, 45, a native of Brigus South on the Southern Shore, was invited to attend the ceremony by Prime Minister Pierre Trudeau's office. He is among a number of Canadians who received special invitations to attend the historical event. The lawyer was singled out because of his accomplishments. He overcame the physical and emotional difficulties experienced by a quadraplegic and went on to obtain a law degree from Dalhousie University in Halifax. Battcock was disabled in 1966 while he was project manager of a hydroelectric project at Baie d'Espoir. Bridge timbers on a backwoods road gave way beneath his vehicle and he was thrown out. He has never walked since and the only movement he has below his neck is in his right hand, and that came only after three years of therapy. Although he is unable to grip anything in his right hand, he is able to operate electronic equipment, including an electric wheelchair which assists him in his legal practice and every day life.

TWENTY-FIVE

Personal Time

DURING THIS PERIOD OF ADRIAN'S LIFE THINGS settled into a comfortable rhythm. He found fulfillment in his work at the Department of Justice, balancing his professional responsibilities with the structure of his daily routines at the Hoyles Home. Content with the pattern his life had taken, Adrian embraced the predictability that came with it, finding joy in the familiar. Fridays were sacred: after a long week, Adrian could always be found with his usual crew at the Law Library, ready for a drink and some laughs. What started as just a "quick one" often spiralled into an evening of storytelling, friendly debates, and—almost without fail—Adrian's off-key but enthusiastic singing. His circle of friends remained strong, offering companionship and lively conversation, while he continued to pursue his passions—none more fervently than his love for politics.

At the time, Canadian politics was an arena of particular interest to Adrian. A prominent figure on his radar was John Crosbie, a fellow Newfoundlander known for his wit, sharp intellect, and outspokenness. In 1983, Crosbie announced his candidacy for the leadership of the Progressive Conservative Party of Canada, a move that captured Adrian's attention. This leadership race marked a significant political moment in Canadian history, and Adrian eagerly followed the developments, discussing the unfolding events with friends and colleagues. Politics, to Adrian, wasn't just a passing interest—it was a source of spirited debate, inspiration, and connection to the larger world beyond his routine.

John Crosbie was a charismatic and influential politician known for his deep devotion to public service. His political career spanned decades, during which he served at both the provincial and federal levels. Crosbie was a key player in major political developments in Canada, advocating fiercely for his home province while earning respect—and sometimes controversy—nationwide. Many considered him to be a leader of the social-liberal wing within the Progressive Conservative Party, often taking stances that were ahead of his time. While many conservatives resisted shifts on social issues, Crosbie openly advocated for the rights of gay and lesbian individuals and took a pro-choice stance on abortion. His progressive views became particularly notable during his tenure as federal Minister of Justice, when his policies and public statements reflected a commitment to human rights and personal freedoms.

Crosbie's genuine interest in people extended beyond politics. He was known to appreciate those who showed integrity and dedication to making a difference. When he learned of Adrian's advocacy efforts—particularly his work advancing social support systems and accessibility—Crosbie sought Adrian's company. Their conversations were spirited and full of mutual respect. Crosbie admired Adrian for his persistence and strong principles, qualities he valued deeply. Whether they talked about policy, advocacy, or the struggles of breaking down barriers, their shared passion for helping others created a strong bond between them.

Adrian was invited to a big fundraising event for John Crosbie at the Newfoundland Hotel, a night full of celebrations with the

St. John's social scene out in full force. The drinks were flowing freely, and it felt like everyone in Newfoundland and Labrador had turned up to show their support for Crosbie. Adrian, never one to waste a good opportunity, got right into the spirit of things. Somewhere, between the third drink and a rousing conversation about politics, someone swears they heard Adrian say, "Forget fundraisers—we should just throw these parties weekly." By the end of the night, Adrian might not have remembered every conversation, but he sure knew he'd had a great time. Although Crosbie's campaign for leadership of the party was bold and garnered significant attention, he narrowly lost to Brian Mulroney. This leadership race was pivotal, as it paved the way for the Progressive Conservatives to defeat the Liberals in the 1984 federal election, ushering in a new era of political change in Canada. Crosbie later held influential federal portfolios, including Minister of Finance, Minister of Fisheries and Oceans, and Minister for International Trade. He left a lasting mark on Canadian politics with his blunt, often humorous style, and was regarded as both a fierce advocate for Newfoundland and a central figure in shaping policy across the country.

One of Adrian's closest friends was Ron Cole, a fellow lawyer at the Justice Department. The two met during their time at law school in Halifax, where Ron was two years behind Adrian. Their friendship quickly grew, and Ron served as an usher at Adrian's graduation. Having both experienced the loss of their fathers at a young age, they shared a deep understanding of the challenges that shaped their lives. They also bonded over their shared passion for human rights and their love of friendly debates, often sparring over differing views for fun—especially over a drink or two. Their professional collaboration was equally meaningful. Together, they worked on several projects to improve accessibility, including a major initiative focused on creating designated handicapped parking spots and amending the Highway Traffic Act. Adrian recognized Ron's efforts at a Canadian Paraplegic Association (CPA) meeting by presenting him with a certificate of appreciation.

Ron's visits were a highlight for Adrian, filled with animated discussions about legal issues, current events, and personal anecdotes. These Sunday afternoon meetups often coincided with a flurry of other callers. Occasionally, Ron would bring along his three young children, much to Adrian's delight. Adrian loved having the kids around, finding their energy refreshing, and he truly valued the time they all spent together.

Ron's daughter, Laura Cole, recalling one visit, wrote the following:

> When I was a kid, 10 years old or so, my dad would take my sisters and me to visit Adrian. He was always happy to see us and introduce us to neighbours and staff along the floor. My sisters and I loved taking turns riding around on the back of his wheelchair. We used to stand on the battery and hang on to the push handles as he drove from his room around the corner to the kitchen. Adrian offered us whatever was available as treats, usually cookies and ice cream dixie cups, which we accepted with delight. He would almost always speak French to encourage us to practice what we had been learning in school. He would ask us our names and how we were doing "*en Français*." And I would do my best to answer correctly. As part of his encouragement, Adrian gave me a French-English dictionary, which I've kept to this day.

Adrian loved keeping up with friends around St. John's and rarely missed a good party. Somehow, he always managed to find his way into the trickiest spots and the most exclusive gatherings, surprising everyone with his determination and sociable nature. Both at the Hoyles Home and at his workplace, holiday celebrations were big events, and he looked forward to joining in. St. Patrick's Day parties were his favourite, where he'd fully embrace the festivities, sharing laughs, singing along with every song and encouraging others to join in.

Regina Sullivan continued to be a constant presence in Adrian's life, not only as a companion but as a caregiver as well. She had a way of making the logistics of his outings—concerts, shows, or just a simple trip out—look effortless. She had stayed in St. John's while he was in Halifax, but they had remained close. Once Adrian returned, she stepped right back into his life. She kept close tabs on his health, worked with staff to address any concerns, and made sure Adrian had the extra help and accommodations he needed. As time went on, Regina took on much of the practical side of his life—buying his clothes, managing his finances, and joining him on outings. For trips outside the home, they usually used the community van. Though the van was always in demand, Adrian somehow got priority. As one staff member said: "Adrian had the driver wrapped around his little finger."

Regina often picked out books she knew Adrian would like and would sit and read to him. She also made music tapes filled with his favourite songs, which always sparked fun conversations. Adrian loved talking about the old days, especially the songs he used to dance to. He'd joke, "You never saw me on the dance floor!" Regina would laugh as he shared stories about sneaking into parties and charming everyone there. On a number of occasions, Adrian reserved the communal room for special gatherings. He and Regina would co-host these events, working together to ensure that everyone felt welcomed and included. He extended invitations not only to his own family but also to Regina's, blending the two circles into one lively, overlapping community. Regina grew very close to Adrian's family over time. She spent many hours with his mother and sisters, and she formed warm, lasting bonds with his nieces and nephews. She was especially generous in helping the younger members of the family find summer employment, using her contacts and initiative to open doors for them. Adrian's niece, Jeanine, fondly recalls the summer Regina helped her secure a position at one of the seniors' homes in St. John's. Regina saw Adrian as her life companion.

During this time, Adrian maintained several romantic relationships. He was careful to coordinate the schedules of all the women in his life so their visits did not overlap. Having multiple partners didn't necessarily diminish the significance of Adrian's connection with Regina, but rather highlighted the breadth and diversity of his social network and the different roles various individuals played in his life. Organizing separate schedules for his female friends allowed him to navigate his relationships in a way that was respectful to everyone involved.

Adrian could often be spotted wheeling through the Avalon Mall, gracefully navigating his way through the aisles of familiar stores. He was on a mission to find the perfect gift for his loved ones, always thoughtful about selecting something meaningful. As he browsed, the van would be parked just outside, patiently waiting for his return. The staff at several of his favourite stores recognized him and were eager to help. Whether it was offering suggestions, showing him the latest items, or assisting him with his selections, they took pleasure in helping him find exactly what he was looking for. When Adrian made his selection, he would have the cashier reach into his breast pocket to retrieve his credit card, then return it along with the receipt.

In his room at the home, Adrian continued to entertain his family and friends in style. With a well-stocked bar and his attendants stepping in as bartenders, he created a cozy social hub where everyone felt welcome and relaxed. As the 1980s drew to a close, Adrian raised a toast. "May the next decade bring even more laughter, music, and a few more wild stories!"

TWENTY-SIX

National Advisory Commission of Employment Equity

IN 1986, PEOPLE WITH DISABILITIES WERE INCLUDED alongside women, visible minorities, and Indigenous People in the new federal Employment Equity Act following the Report of the Royal Commission on Equality in Employment.

In 1988, Adrian was appointed to the National Advisory Commission of Employment Equity to the President of the Treasury Board and for one year served as chairman. The Employment Equity Act is a key element of the legislative authority that ensures equity and justice in the public service. Under the Act, the employer is required to measure progress in terms of representation and continually improve the workplace experience with respect to employment equity.

The core public administration is responsible for making targeted efforts to ensure that the public service meets or exceeds the workforce availability of these designated groups. The

Commission was responsible for overseeing the development of the employment equity plan by setting targets that align with the Act. After the development phase, the committee oversaw the development of policies and procedures that ensured compliance with the Act as well as the Labour Relations Act. Each year, the President of the Treasury Board of Canada presents a comprehensive annual report to Parliament concerning employment equity within the Public Service of Canada. This report serves as a critical tool for assessing the progress and outcomes of employment equity initiatives across various federal departments and agencies. It includes detailed analyses of demographic representation, recruitment, retention, and promotion practices to ensure fairness and equity in employment opportunities.

Moreover, the report highlights achievements, challenges, and future priorities in advancing inclusion and employment equity goals within the public sector. It provides transparency on government efforts to promote representation and accessibility for groups historically underrepresented in the workforce.

During Adrian's tenure on the National Advisory Commission, he helped develop employment equity strategies and shape policies to promote diversity and inclusivity in the workplace. Operating at the intersection of provincial and federal entities on employment equity, Adrian facilitated the exchange of ideas and strategies between these two levels of government, fostering collaboration that led to more comprehensive and effective initiatives nationwide. His efforts contributed significantly to advancing equal opportunities for individuals with disabilities in the workforce. According to Adrian: "Education is the linchpin upon which the future aspirations of all disabled people rest." He saw education as one of the best ways of breaking down the barriers—physical and attitudinal—that exist between the disabled and the non-disabled.

In the latter part of the 1980s, there were several initiatives to promote employment equity in the province. Perhaps the best known and most effective was the Vocational Rehabilitation Professional Development Program (VRPD), which offered financial assistance for individuals with disabilities to pursue higher education. There were a few strong allies within government who worked tirelessly behind the scenes to ensure the success of these initiatives. Their support was crucial in advancing opportunities for disabled individuals in the work force.

In the 1990s, amidst federal and provincial governments implementing deficit reduction strategies including cuts to social programs, the provincial government made the decision to cut the VRPD program. This action prompted all advocacy groups concerned with disability rights to unite in opposition to the cuts. Through a robust and coordinated campaign, they successfully overturned the decision, ensuring continued access to essential educational and vocational support for individuals with disabilities in the province.

Despite the endorsement of the social model of disability—which suggests that people are disabled by systemic barriers and negative perceptions rather than by their disability—numerous advances in treatment and assistive technology, and commitment by governments to social equality and inclusion, there are still real concerns in ensuring meaningful labour-market participation for individuals with disabilities in this country. Persons with disabilities have traditionally struggled to achieve economic independence through employment, mostly because they have been perceived as objects of care and dependent individuals who require societal protection and support to compensate for their disabilities. Today, within the Government of Newfoundland and Labrador, there is an Office of Employment Equity for persons with

Disabilities (OEEPD). It operates several employment programs and career development services to assist persons with disabilities to obtain employment in provincial government departments.

Adrian's involvement in numerous boards, agencies, and committees highlighted his steadfast dedication to making real change. He presented to a variety of influential groups, including the Equality Rights Committee, the Liberal Task Force Committee on Employment and Unemployment, and the Provincial Royal Commission on Employment and Unemployment. Through these platforms, he pushed to bring issues of disability rights and accessibility into the heart of public policy conversations. In each of these public engagements, he worked to raise awareness about the barriers faced by people with disabilities. He used personal stories to make the issues more relatable, helping others understand the urgency of addressing these situations. His presentations weren't just informative; they were calls to action. For instance, during his time at the Provincial Royal Commission on Employment and Unemployment, his carefully considered recommendations were accepted unanimously.

Adrian's passion for a more inclusive society inspired others to join the movement for equality. Speaking with honesty and conviction, he influenced lawmakers and encouraged individuals with disabilities to stand up for their rights. His advocacy wasn't limited to speeches and recommendations; he also worked behind the scenes, quietly pushing for services that had been previously unavailable. One notable success was his advocacy for free cable television systems in local institutions, giving many people with disabilities better access to information and entertainment. Through all of his efforts, Adrian remained a powerful force for positive change. He usually reinforced his mission with a powerful mantra he shared in his presentations: "The level of sophistication of a society is judged by how their disabled are treated." This guiding principle fuelled his work, helping to transform attitudes and policies, leaving a lasting impact on the communities he served.

In the later part of the twentieth century, a combination of changes helped bring more attention to people with disabilities and sparked a shift in attitudes, improving lives in significant ways. One of the major changes came with the development of new assistive technologies, especially wheelchairs. These newer models were much more advanced than what had come before, providing people with greater mobility and independence. Modern wheelchairs were designed with better materials that were lighter and easier to manoeuvre, making it possible for users to navigate different terrains, both indoors and outdoors, more easily. They also included important features like power-assisted wheels, adjustable seating, and improved suspension systems, all of which made using them much more comfortable and efficient. These improvements meant that people who had difficulty moving around could now participate more fully in activities like social events, education, and work. It was a major step forward in breaking down the physical barriers that had previously limited their opportunities to take part in everyday life.

This progress in technology not only made life more comfortable for individuals but also helped increase their sense of independence. It played a key role in empowering people with disabilities to feel more included and able to engage with the wider community. As technology improved, it made it easier for people to live more autonomous lives, and that change had a ripple effect in transforming how society viewed and interacted with those with disabilities. For Adrian, witnessing these advances first-hand reinforced his belief in practical solutions and strengthened his commitment to creating opportunities that allowed people to participate fully in both work and community life.

In 1992, Adrian was awarded the Commemorative Medal for the 125th Anniversary of Canadian Confederation. The medal recognized Adrian for his significant contributions to Canada and his work helping others. It highlighted his lifelong devotion to community service and his efforts to promote disability advocacy and social inclusion across the country.

Adrian's friend, Ron Cole, was a strong supporter of Adrian's work. He played a key role in recommending Adrian for the Order of Canada and helped with his nomination for a spot on the Board of Regents at Memorial University in 1984. As part of the process, Adrian wrote a heartfelt statement about his time at Memorial as a student with a disability. He thanked the faculty and fellow students who had supported him but also pointed out the ongoing barriers disabled students faced on campus. In his statement, Adrian urged Memorial University to do more for accessibility, asking for better accommodations and resources for students with disabilities. He highlighted the need to tackle physical barriers and the larger institutional challenges to make the campus truly inclusive. His goal was simple: he wanted changes that would help future students have equal opportunities and improve the overall educational experience for everyone.

Adrian was chosen as the alumni representative and served on both the Board's Appointments and Arts Committees. Being elected to the Board of Regents was a big achievement for Adrian, and he took the responsibility seriously, knowing he had to represent and advocate for both alumni and current students. His role gave him the chance to speak up and share his perspective, shaped by his own experience as a student with a disability. His presence on the Board sparked important discussions about equality, and he used his position to push for changes that would make Memorial University a more welcoming and supportive place for all students.

When Adrian served on the Board of Regents, their meetings were held on the second floor of the Arts and Administration Building, which didn't have an elevator. As the first person in a wheelchair to serve on the Board, Adrian's presence led the university to install an elevator so he could attend the meetings. When Adrian was appointed to the Board, it felt like a fitting turn of events. The same staff member who had told him back in 1969, "If you can't write, you can't attend Memorial University," was still working there. Now, Adrian had moved into an important leadership role at the very institution that had once doubted him. He never confronted the remark directly, but he never forgot it either. Instead, he transformed it into humour, often joking when asked for his biography, "I'm the only lawyer in North America who can't write."

TWENTY-SEVEN

The Hoyles Home in the 1980s & 1990s

THE CONSTANT STREAM OF GUESTS TO ADRIAN'S room at the Hoyles Home was a clear indication of how deeply Adrian was loved. The room where he lived for nearly two decades was his sanctuary—a place of comfort, security, and individuality. Friends and family took great care in decorating Adrian's room, filling it with meaningful items and mementoes that made it feel like his own. His bookcases were lined with his vast collection of law books, reflecting his deep passion for his career, but they also housed a variety of other literary works that spoke to his wide range of interests. The room was personalized with pieces of his life—family photographs, memorabilia, and keepsakes from his travels and experiences. Among these items was a scrapbook he kept, filled with newspaper clippings, photographs, greeting cards, and notes. Each page held a reminder of special moments that had shaped his life.

Adrian had insisted from the start on a private room, a request that was readily granted. This private setting allowed him to maintain the personal autonomy he valued, with certain freedoms that helped him feel both independent and connected to his sense of self. One of these liberties was the ability to keep alcohol in his room, which he enjoyed sharing with friends and guests.

Friday nights were time for the family to visit, usually with a meal in hand. Saturday nights were Adrian's own. If a visitor arrived, Adrian noted the visit and very quickly ushered the person out of the room. While the specific activities of Saturday nights remained undisclosed, the fact was Adrian wanted personal time and space. This boundary communicated that there were aspects of his life he preferred to keep separate from social interactions. Ultimately, it reflected Adrian's desire for balance. Though Adrian's door was often open to friends and family, he valued solitude too. There were times when he preferred to be alone, to reflect or simply recharge, and the Hoyles Home staff honoured this need for privacy, granting him the quiet space he required. This balance—between noisy gatherings and cherished solitude—helped Adrian cultivate a life of both connection and personal freedom within his own room.

While he valued quiet moments to himself, Adrian also found companionship in other, less demanding ways. He loved watching television. He regularly watched political shows and news broadcasts to stay updated on current events. A friend had set up a VCR for him so he could watch movies more easily, and his nephew would load up old films to make sure they were ready to go. Adrian had a soft spot for classic adventure films, and one of his all-time favourites was *The Great Train Robbery*, a movie he watched over and over. He was especially into sports, following his favourite teams and keeping up with the latest games, which likely tied back to his own love for athletics. The NHL playoffs were the highlight of the year. Again, his room was the place to be—a Habs fan to the end. As much as he loved them, their gradual decline from dominance tormented him. While he followed the scores and seasons closely, it was his own family and friends who truly captured his attention.

Adrian was deeply devoted to his nieces and nephews, building relationships that were as meaningful as they were enduring. He was generous not only with gifts but also with his time and advice. Whether they sought guidance on their careers, education, or personal lives, Adrian's wisdom and insight were always available. He never missed their birthdays or special occasions, marking each milestone with thoughtful gifts that reflected his attention to their personalities and interests. In addition to his generosity, Adrian's sense of humour made him a favourite among the younger generation. His quick wit and funny stories always had everyone laughing, and some of his tales became well-loved family memories. Beyond the laughter, Adrian imparted important life lessons. One particular piece of advice stood out and became a guiding principle for many of them: "Make sure you make your own decisions." This encouragement to think independently and take charge of their lives left a lasting impression on them.

A visit from a niece or nephew was always welcomed. When it was time for them to leave, he would send them off with a reminder: "Check the pocket of my jacket; I have something for you." Without fail, they would find a $100 bill tucked inside. It became a signature gesture of his generosity. Adrian always made sure to visit the bank ahead of time, ensuring he had that specific denomination on hand, just for them. His niece JoAnn (Battcock) O'Brien relates the following story:

> On one of my visits to Hoyles Home, Uncle Adrian directed me to get something from his dresser. This wasn't unusual, as when family and friends visited, he might ask someone to get

> a bottle and have a toddy with him. This request, I was soon to discover, was for a different purpose. It was November 1983, and I was twenty years old, living in MUN's Burton's Pond Apartments, and in the last year of studies for my science degree. Uncle Adrian told me to find an envelope in the drawer with my name on it, and said it was to help with my studies. I opened the envelope and saw that it contained ten $100 bills—$1,000. Wow!!! As a university student on a fixed budget, I was overwhelmed by this generosity.

JoAnn continues:

> But I was most deeply affected by the next thing he asked of me. He directed me to take a crafted butterfly picture from the wall and dictated this message, which I was to scribe on the back of the wall hanging—"to a very special niece, work hard, think well of everyone—like your father and I. Realise that we are all on the human concourse together. Give and take, but balance interests. Remember to temper any judgement or decision with humanity. Love Uncle Adrian."

JoAnn concluded, "these were words of wisdom for sure, and values that I believe lived with him and Dad [Junior Battcock], and Uncle Bob [Bob McGrath, Adrian's friend and brother-in-law] their entire lives. How fortunate we were/are to have had these role models in our lives."

Time with visitors was always special, but the demands of daily life at the Hoyles Home quickly resumed. His day would start at 6:30 a.m. when two attendants would help him get out of bed using a hoist lift. After his personal care they would help him pick out clothes for the day and get dressed. Adrian was very particular about his clothing, so the caregivers made sure to choose outfits he liked and felt comfortable in. He always liked to wear a sweater or vest with a pocket. He could carry things like a comb, credit cards, money, a pencil, et cetera in the pocket. While Adrian couldn't physically reach for them, having these essentials close by gave him a sense of preparedness and control. Following that, he would need help with eating and taking his medications, while the staff would keep an eye on his food intake to make sure he was getting enough nutrition and hydration. They would also look out for any signs of health issues related to his condition and notify the medical team if needed.

Around 9 a.m., Adrian would leave for work. His work schedule was limited to mornings only and tailored to accommodate his physical abilities. The remainder of the day would include any treatments or therapies as prescribed and personal time with any number of visits from family and friends.

After his accident, Adrian had developed serious bedsores that were difficult to treat. He had many other physical challenges that required constant attention from the medical staff. He also had a permanent catheter that needed regular monitoring and care to prevent infections and other issues. Over time, Adrian became more aware of the steps needed to protect his body and prevent further problems. Along with the care provided at the Hoyles Home, he hired a private physiotherapist to make sure he received the best possible treatment. He worked hard to take care of his health and well-being, showing his determination to stay as independent as he could.

Despite being careful, Adrian often dealt with health problems. He regularly caught colds and the flu, which took a long time to get over. He also had a few surgeries for internal issues. On one occasion, both his hands were badly burned. A staff member had placed them in boiling water as part of a care routine without testing the temperature, and had left briefly to attend to another matter. Because Adrian couldn't feel the heat and couldn't pull his hands away, the burns were severe. Due to circulation problems, they took a long time to heal, forcing him to take time off work. These health incidents were hard, but Adrian dealt with them as best he could. Adrian's professional experience and advocacy work meant that fellow residents at the Hoyles Home often turned to him with questions about legislation and disability rights. He actively taught residents about their rights, encouraging them to speak up and assert themselves. Dedicated to boosting their confidence, Adrian consistently answered questions and offered guidance. Adrian often declared, "Everyone here deserves respect, no exceptions," urging, "Speak up—your voice matters as much as anyone else's." His unwavering advocacy occasionally clashed with senior staff, who found his influence aggressive, but Adrian remained steadfast in ensuring every resident was heard and valued.

When the Escasoni Place group home was established, Adrian was offered a place, but he declined. For a time, he and Regina even considered buying a house and setting up a home together so that they could live more independently. As noted earlier, Adrian was deeply touched by her willingness to take on that responsibility. Yet, after much reflection, he came to realize that the physical demands and constant care his condition required would place too heavy a burden on her. In the end, he chose to remain at the Hoyles Home. Despite its shortcomings, it was the place he had come to regard as home, and he resolved, as he so often did, to make the best of it.

The staff at the Home went out of their way to make special occasions truly memorable, and Adrian always looked forward to them, especially birthdays and holidays. Christmas, in particular, stirred a deep sense of nostalgia in him. The Home would be transformed with festive decorations, and choirs from local churches came to sing traditional carols, something Adrian loved. In many ways, it was the preparations for Christmas that brought back memories of the happy seasons he had spent years earlier at Mount Cashel—since he had been away with family during the actual holidays—which made the time leading up to Christmas at the Hoyles Home all the more meaningful to him. In his own way, he made sure to spread holiday cheer as well. Each year, he carefully prepared gifts for the staff, and on Christmas Eve they would gather in his room for a small celebration, exchanging presents and sharing a toast with a drop of holiday cheer.

TWENTY-EIGHT

Criminal Injuries Compensation Board

IN 1990, ADRIAN WAS NAMED CHAIRMAN OF THE Newfoundland Criminal Injuries Compensation Board. In making the announcement, Justice Minister Paul Dicks said, "Mr. Battcock will bring a wealth of experience and understanding to his new position as full-time chairman." His appointment signified a profound trust in his integrity, judgment, and ability to navigate sensitive and complex matters. In this role, he oversaw the administration of funds to victims of crime, ensuring that they received the support and assistance they needed to cope with the aftermath of traumatic experiences.

The Criminal Injuries Compensation Board, established in the early 1970s under provincial legislation, addressed cases involving injuries resulting from criminal acts. These ranged from assaults against wildlife enforcement officers by poachers to taxi drivers attacked by passengers, and other similar incidents. By the late 1980s, the Board began handling applications from victims of crimes committed by members of the clergy, reflecting a shift in the types of cases being brought forward as awareness and reporting of such crimes increased.

Adrian's appointment as chair came at a pivotal time, coinciding with increased attention and demand for its services following the recommendations of the Hughes Inquiry. The Hughes Inquiry, a royal commission, chaired by Judge Samuel Hughes, was initiated after allegations of sexual abuse by members of the Congregation of Christian Brothers against the children in their care at Mount Cashel Orphanage. The inquiry concluded that officials had transferred offenders and covered up the sexual abuse at Mount Cashel, ultimately recommending compensation for the victims, who could also launch civil actions. Many did.

In its first year, the Board saw cases involving assaults and similar crimes committed by clergy members and other individuals in positions of trust. These cases later expanded to include applications from survivors of Mount Cashel, reflecting a broader focus on institutional abuse.

Alongside Adrian, lawyers James Fardy and Colleen Hanrahan also served as members. This was a period of increased demand, and the Board was tasked with handling a large number of inquiries and applications. The members worked closely together, and over time the process was simplified, which helped make it easier for victims to navigate. Clients would present their cases before the Board during morning sessions, with two of the three lawyers required to be present at each session. Colleen Hanrahan noted that despite the often poignant and difficult narratives they encountered, all three members shared an acute recognition of the vulnerability of the clients, and treated each individual with utmost respect. The Board was allocated an office outside the Confederation Building, deliberately separated from the broader operations of the Justice Department to streamline convenience for the clients.

Adrian's association with the commission tasked with compensating the victims of Mount Cashel likely presented a complex and emotionally difficult situation for him. His connection to the orphanage, coupled with his deep respect and high regard for the Christian Brothers there, would have made the process of confronting and addressing the abuses that occurred particularly difficult. Yet, Adrian's ability to navigate this delicate situation with empathy and an unwavering commitment to justice speaks volumes about his character. Adrian's colleagues were unaware that he had grown up in Mount Cashel, which speaks to his high level of professionalism and ability to separate his personal experiences from his professional duties.

Everyone in the office struggled to comprehend and come to terms with the harrowing details of these cases. As the Mount Cashel abuses gained public attention, other instances of clergy abuse also surfaced. The revelations triggered a profound shift in the community of St. John's, and across Newfoundland as a whole, where suddenly the trust in clergy was shattered, and suspicion took its place. The world in which they had lived was irrevocably changed, making the work even more challenging for those on the Board.

Adrian's friend, Paul Dicks, who had become the Minister of Justice, often met with him during his official duties. Adrian frequently pointed out how inaccessible the Supreme Court building was, even though accommodations were made for him on the rare occasions he visited. After many discussions with Adrian, Paul decided to take action. He secured government funding and oversaw the construction of a large ramp on the Duckworth Street side of the building, which was named the Adrian Battcock Ramp. After Adrian passed away, a plaque was placed there to honour his efforts in advocating for accessibility.

Adrian valued his time at the Criminal Injuries Compensation Board. He appreciated the convenience of their separate offices on Elizabeth Avenue, which were much more accessible for him than the larger and more formal Confederation Building. The smaller, close-knit team made the work environment enjoyable, and he found real satisfaction in the meaningful work they accomplished together. What he especially loved about the Elizabeth Avenue location was how easily friends and family could stop by for a visit. Unlike the formalities of the Confederation Building, the office was open and welcoming, allowing Adrian to host impromptu visits. His sisters, nieces, and nephews often dropped in, and he would greet them with enthusiasm. Sometimes his sister Carmel would bring their mother, Maggie, for a visit. In her late nineties and with limited mobility, Maggie was living at St. Patrick's Mercy Home, where she had moved in 1990, making these moments with her all the more meaningful.

Adrian was disappointed when the government decided to dissolve the Criminal Injuries Compensation Board and integrate the work into the Victim Services Division. He returned to the Department of Justice at the Confederation Building in the Spring of 1993 as senior solicitor.

In his professional capacity, Adrian was often sought after for more than just legal counsel. His extensive knowledge and experience made him a valuable resource for those navigating complex legal issues. However, his role extended far beyond formal legal advice. He was a mentor who provided career guidance, helping individuals chart their paths and make informed decisions about their futures. His dedication to others wasn't confined to professional matters, however. Adrian was also known for his personal support. The staff at the Hoyles Home affectionately referred to him as the resident counsellor. He was approachable and willing to share his own experiences and struggles, particularly regarding his disability. Adrian spoke openly about coming to terms with his situation, how his personal journey shaped his approach to life, and his interactions with others.

He often talked about the importance of acceptance and being kind to yourself. He shared how his life became so much easier once he stopped fighting against his circumstances and learned to embrace them. His words struck a chord with people because he didn't just talk about it—he lived it. Adrian showed everyone around him how powerful it could be to accept yourself and find peace within, no matter the challenges you face. Ambition was nothing new to Adrian; he had always been driven to make something of his life. After the accident, however, that drive took on a new direction. He discovered a deeper sense of purpose and began to focus less on his earlier pursuits and more on making a real difference in the lives of others.

Adrian's legacy isn't just the stories people tell about him—it's also the lasting difference he made in people's lives. He combined his knowledge and skills with genuine care and the powerful lessons he shared about finding acceptance and purpose. Adrian had a special way of connecting with and inspiring those around him, leaving a deep impression on everyone he met.

TWENTY-NINE

A Special Protégé

WHILE STUDYING AT MEMORIAL UNIVERSITY during the 1980s, Sean FitzGerald worked as an untrained orderly at the Hoyles Home. It was here that he met Adrian, an encounter that would profoundly shape his life. Early in his tenure at the Hoyles Home, Adrian took a special interest in Sean, addressing him as "my son." This paternal approach fostered a deep and enduring bond between them. Adrian became a mentor to Sean, taking a keen interest in his personal life, academic pursuits, and future career. He offered thoughtful advice and guidance, which greatly influenced Sean, who was young and impressionable at the time. Sean admired Adrian, viewing him as a father figure and a source of inspiration.

Their relationship extended beyond the confines of the Hoyles Home. On Sean's days off, he would frequently visit Adrian, and often they would go to the Holiday Inn for a meal. These shared meals were more than just a break from work; they were opportunities for Sean to learn from Adrian's wisdom. Sean was especially interested in Adrian's views on general health care and rehabilitation services in the province. Recognizing Sean's enthusiasm and potential, Adrian eventually recommended that Sean run for a position on the Board of Directors of the Hoyles Home, a suggestion that Sean followed. Once on the board, Sean leveraged his extensive work experience to contribute significantly. After Sean completed his degree, Adrian recommended that he apply for the position of Executive Director with the Canadian Paraplegic Association (CPA). Adrian provided thorough preparation for the interview, ensuring Sean was well equipped for the challenge. Despite the strong competition from many candidates, Sean secured the job, a testament to the solid guidance he received. At the time of his hiring, he was just twenty-four years old.

The Newfoundland branch of the CPA had been established in the mid-1970s providing crucial support and advocacy for individuals with spinal cord injuries. When Sean FitzGerald took over in the later part of the 1980s, he expanded its reach and impact. Branch offices were opened and regional staff were hired. Under his guidance, CPA Newfoundland and Labrador grew from one office and three staff, with an annual budget of $176,000, to twelve offices and almost one hundred employees, and an annual budget of over $2 million. Additionally, during this time CPA spearheaded the building of two accessible housing complexes.

During Sean's time at the CPA, he leaned heavily on Adrian for his guidance and expertise. Adrian's dedication to the organization and his deep understanding of disability-related challenges made him an invaluable resource. Whether it was helping to design programs, advising on outreach efforts, or supporting clients directly, Adrian's contributions were essential to advancing the CPA's mission.

Over time, the CPA grew and evolved into Spinal Cord Injury Newfoundland and Labrador, continuing its work to help individuals with spinal cord injuries achieve independence, self-reliance, and full participation in their communities. Adrian's commitment to this mission remained unwavering. At the time of his passing, he was serving as chairman of the Board of Directors, a role that reflected his lifelong dedication to empowering others and driving meaningful change.

Sean FitzGerald transitioned through numerous roles and positions in his career, maintaining a close relationship with Adrian until Adrian's death. Sean cherished their enduring friendship and valued Adrian's mentorship, which shaped his own contributions to the field. Adrian's passing left a void in Sean's life, yet his influence continued to inspire Sean's dedication to advocating for disability rights and improving the lives of others. When Sean and his wife had their first son, they named him Adrian in honour of his dear friend.

Sean is just one of the many individuals whose lives were profoundly influenced by Adrian. He surrounded himself with a diverse group of people, offering his wisdom and support in various aspects of their lives. His effect of them was profound and multifaceted, extending well beyond the examples of his career. Known for his wisdom and empathy, Adrian became a trusted confidant for many, offering advice and a compassionate ear to those seeking direction in their lives.

Adrian's sister Sheila visiting her mother's and brother's graves. The family always called the Mass at Holy Sepulchre cemetery "The Garden Party". They would go early and bring a snack and a chair for the Mass, and reconnect with family and friends.

In July, 1994, Adrian's family (brother John, sister-in-law Sheila, sisters Sheila and Carmel) visited Grand Falls for the official opening of Battcock Manor, a supportive and accessible housing complex.

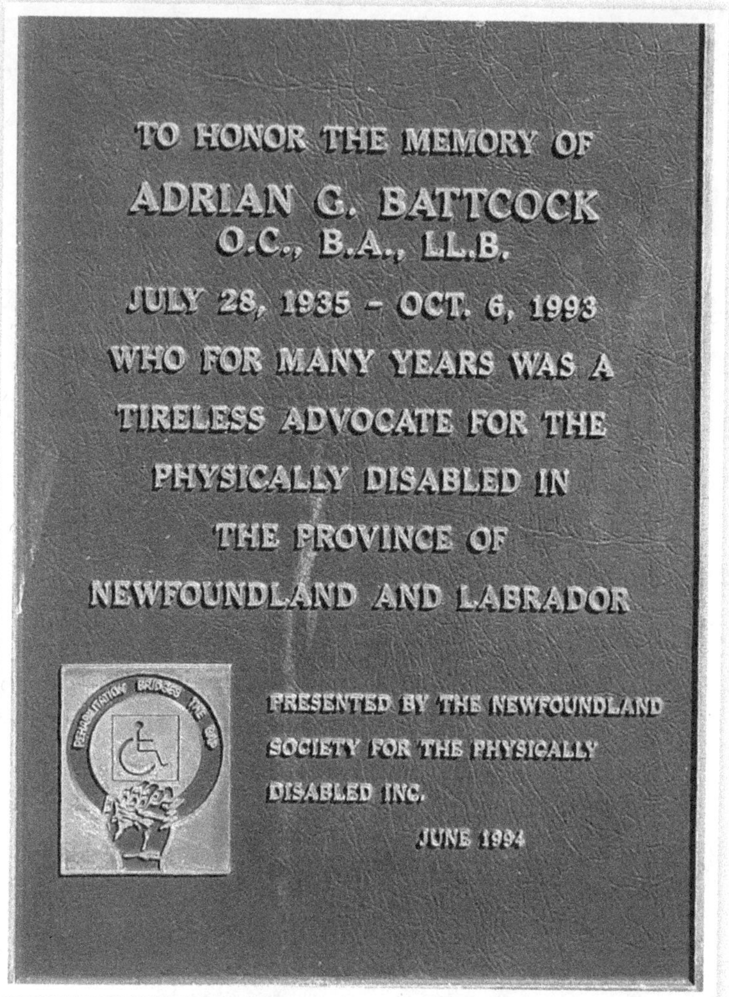

A plaque honoring Adrian installed at the Supreme Court building in St. John's, Newfoundland. Located at the entrance to the wheelchair-accessible ramp, this tribute serves as a lasting reminder of his many contributions and the respect he earned throughout his life.

A tribute to Adrian Battcock

Colleagues and friends were saddened to learn of the sudden passing of Adrian Battcock from cancer October 6. Adrian was a solicitor in the Department of Justice from 1977 until his death. He was also Chairman of the Newfoundland Crimes Compensation Board and Chairman of the Board of the Canadian Paraplegic Association (Newfoundland and Labrador) Inc.

> *"Barriers are obstacles for one to overcome, and obstacles are challenges we must face head-on."*
> – Adrian Battcock

Premier Clyde Wells paid public tribute to Adrian, saying: "Throughout his life, Adrian demonstrated that the only boundaries we face in life are the ones we set for ourselves... By his quiet efforts, he was able to improve the quality of life for disabled people in Newfoundland and Labrador."

Justice minister, Ed Roberts said: "Adrian will be missed by everyone who knew him. His unfailing good nature and infectious humour touched all who worked with him in every facet of his life... We are all better for having known him..."

A man of action

During the 1960s, Adrian was a captain in the Special Services with the United Nations Peace Keeping Force in Africa. After his discharge, he took a position as camp manager at the hydroelectric project in Baie d'Espoir. In 1966, a temporary bridge on a construction road collapsed under his vehicle, sending it into the river. Adrian never walked again. After three years of determination and extensive physiotherapy, he regained limited use of his right arm. He was unable to grip anything, but managed to control his specially adapted wheelchair and telephone.

In 1969, Adrian enrolled at Memorial University, graduating in 1973 with a bachelor of arts (psychology). In 1974, he was admitted to the Faculty of Law at Dalhousie University, where he assisted Dr. Donald Curran, helping to prepare and present modern legislation affecting the disabled in Nova Scotia.

He graduated in 1976 with a bachelor of law, returned to Newfoundland and articled under the Deputy Minister of Justice, the late Vincent P. McCarthy, Q.C. Adrian was called to the bar in May 1977, and acted as counsel to several government departments. He became Chairman of the Crimes Compensation Board, which he spearheaded at the request of then-minister Paul Dicks, in 1990.

Meeting the challenge head-on

Adrian was always active in improving the quality of life for persons with disabilities. He was a member of Terra Transport's Management Advisory Board for the Province of Newfoundland. This board introduced a provincial bus system with wheelchair capability. The project was so successful it was followed across Canada, the United States and other jurisdictions.

Other examples of his legacy include the implementation of the Buildings Accessibility Act, and improved benefits for seniors. While on the board of regents at Memorial University, Adrian was instrumental in making Memorial one of the most accesssible universities in Canada.

In recognition of these achievements, he received the Canadian Paraplegic Association's Paraplegic of the Year Award, the C.A. Pippy Award for Handicapped Person of the Year, and a Canada 125 Commemorative Medal. Adrian was also inducted into the Order of Canada.

Adrian was no stranger to parliamentary committees, royal task forces, royal commissions, and senate committee hearings. His presentations, comments and input were professional and logical, and many times one can find his recommendations in current legislation and policy.

Adrian's vision was the creation of an environment which would be accessible to every citizen of the country. He said: "Barriers are obstacles for one to overcome, and obstacles are challenges we must face head-on." Adrian leaves to mourn his mother, family, friends and co-workers.

THIRTY

The End

UNTIL 1990, WHEN MAGGIE'S HEALTH DECLINED, life in Brigus South went on with Maggie and Henry tending to the home together. Maggie often visited her children in St. John's and occasionally travelled outside the province. Henry stayed busy fishing, tending to the garden, and handling any minor repairs around the house. He believed that staying active kept him both physically and mentally sharp, and he found peace in these daily routines.

In 1990, however, it became clear that Maggie could no longer manage in her own home. With most of her children and grandchildren now living in St. John's, it made sense for her to move closer to them. Both Sheila and Carmel offered to take her in, but Maggie hesitated. She didn't want to disrupt their lives or feel like a burden, and she struggled with the idea of leaving her home behind. Despite her concerns, the family knew it was time for Maggie to be closer to them for her well-being.

Arrangements were made for Maggie to move into St. Patrick's Mercy Home, a long-term care facility. She received a cancer diagnosis, and given her advanced age, medical professionals determined that surgery would pose significant risks to Maggie's well-being. Despite this, Dr. Hanna, a family friend who knew Maggie well, agreed to perform the procedure. According to family accounts, Dr. Hanna candidly told her, "If your heart gives out on the table, there's nothing I can do about it." Maggie, undeterred, reportedly replied with characteristic determination, "You look after the cancer, and I'll look after my heart." Remarkably, at the age of ninety-six, she underwent the procedure, which proved to be a resounding success, granting her another five years of life.

When Maggie left Brigus South to move to St. John's, Henry chose to stay in his home, despite the family arranging for him to move into a retirement facility. He was determined to spend his remaining years in the house where he had built his life. He stuck to his routine, with neighbours kindly keeping an eye on him and offering help when needed. Carmel often received calls from the neighbours, saying Henry was up on the roof. There was little she could do to stop him—he insisted he needed to fix leaks and take care of regular maintenance.

However, Henry's health began to decline. Eventually, he agreed to move to St. John's, where he alternated living between Carmel and Sheila's homes. Just weeks later, he suffered a stroke and was taken to the Miller Centre, where he passed away in January 1993 at the age of ninety-four. Henry was the first of three family members to pass that year. During his final days at the Miller Centre, Henry was deeply concerned about the fate of the family home in Brigus South. However, his worries were alleviated when Adrian arrived and assured him that everything was taken care of and that the home would remain in the family, safe and cared for. Surrounded by his loving family, he spent his last hours receiving the care and support he needed. Henry was buried in the Cape Broyle graveyard, next to his parents, and surrounded by ironwork made in the family forge. A quiet and gentle man, he had rarely left his home on the Southern Shore, except for a brief period in New York City. His spirit would surely be content in this peaceful resting place.

In February 1993, the family suffered another devastating loss when Adrian's niece, Anne Marie Buckingham, died in a tragic accident in Ontario. Anne Marie, the daughter of his sister Carmel, was only 30 years old and had been living in Ontario for several years. Her sudden death shocked everyone, but it was especially hard on her cousin Jeanine, who was her closest friend and had also relocated to Ontario. Jeanine received a call from the police, asking her to come and identify the body. She recalls walking into the hospital when a staff member approached her, saying, "You must be related—you look just like her." Jeanine arranged with a funeral home to bring Anne Marie home for burial. It was almost impossible to comprehend that someone so young, with such a bright future ahead, could be gone so suddenly. For a family that had already faced so much together, this loss was an especially heavy blow.

After Anne Marie's death, the family navigated the painful process of planning the wake and funeral, each step a sombre opportunity to reflect on her life. Throughout this time, Adrian was a steady source of support for his sister Carmel. As they came together to mourn, Adrian's presence was a comfort, helping everyone cope with the loss. In the weeks that followed, Adrian became even more attuned to his family's grief. He made frequent calls to check in on his sister and nieces, offering emotional support and a sense of reassurance. His thoughtful attentiveness made it easier for them to manage their sorrow and begin healing together. Little did they realise that in less than eight months, they would be planning Adrian's funeral.

It was Chris Underhay, Adrian's long-time caregiver, who first felt that things were not well with Adrian. He had noticed subtle changes in his demeanour and energy levels. In Adrian's case, where his quadriplegia limited his ability to detect changes in his own well-being, Chris's observations were critical. The tests that followed proved that Chris's concerns were accurate. Adrian's health was declining. His resilience in living with quadriplegia for over twenty-five years had been extraordinary, and the news of his declining health undoubtedly was heartbreaking for everyone who cared about him.

When he was given the diagnosis of cancer, Adrian remarked to his friend Sean, "Hopefully I'll get two or three more years out of it. I've got so much to do." This response starkly contrasted his outlook in the early days following his accident. Back then, his future seemed bleak and he didn't see any path forward for himself. Adrian now saw his remaining time as an opportunity to accomplish unfinished goals and continue his journey with a renewed sense of urgency and focus. However, this was not to be. The aggressive nature of his illness advanced more rapidly than anyone had anticipated. The swift progression of the cancer left little time for the interventions that might have extended his life. He quipped to his nephew, "I always thought it would be the lungs that would take me out."

Adrian had continued to be interested in politics, and even in his final days, his curiosity about the political landscape remained undiminished. In the fall of 1993, Canada was in the midst of a heated election campaign. The Progressive Conservative Party, led by Kim Campbell, was locked in a fierce battle with the Liberal Party, headed by Jean Chrétien. Adrian was a passionate supporter of Chrétien, and during a conversation with his niece, he expressed strong opinions on why he believed the Liberal leader was the strongest candidate for Prime Minister. Although Adrian passed away just two weeks before the election, on October 25, 1993, Jean

Chrétien went on to win, marking a significant shift in Canadian politics. Adrian's keen political insight and his unwavering interest in the country's direction were evident until the very end.

It's never easy to confront the reality of a loved one's declining health, particularly after such a long period of living with significant problems, but his family and friends rallied, determined to ensure his final days were as pleasant as possible. Extended family members and other friends were notified of his imminent death.

Adrian requested that his brother bring his mother, now ninety-seven years old, for a visit. When she arrived, the staff noticed that Adrian had refrained from taking any pain medication since midnight so that he could be fully alert for her visit. In a barely audible voice, he asked her if she needed anything, to which she quietly replied, "No." Their visit was brief, with both understanding it would be their last. Adrian's concern for his mother in that moment not only demonstrated his deep love and care for her, but also his ongoing commitment to her comfort and happiness, even as he faced his own final moments.

Despite the gravity of the situation, there was a touch of humour during their visit. Adrian's mother was hard of hearing, though she never admitted it, and Adrian spoke in a very low voice. Because of this, they needed someone to act as a go-between—Adrian's niece, Jeanine, filled this role. Although living in Toronto Jeanine spent a great deal of time in Newfoundland following the death of her cousin. Adrian would ask his mother if she needed anything, but she often misheard the question and responded with answers that didn't quite fit, brightening their poignant farewell.

When Adrian was transferred to the Health Sciences Centre, he knew this move would be his last. As he was being transported, he made a special request: he wanted to stop by the Department of Justice to say a proper goodbye to his colleagues of the past sixteen years. As he entered the office one last time, emotions ran high. His colleagues gathered around him, reminiscing about their time together, sharing laughs and heartfelt gratitude for the impact Adrian had made. For Adrian, this final reunion was a moment to express his appreciation for their support, camaraderie, and the experiences they had shared.

Family and friends kept vigil during his final hours, taking turns sitting by the bedside. It was an opportunity to share memories, express love, and say goodbye. Even amid the sorrow, there was a quiet sense of peace and closeness—the bond among those present was strong and tangible. Jeanine remembers how, while the family gathered around him, Regina cared for Adrian with gentle attention, cooling his lips with wet sponges and running her fingers through his hair. She could see the anguish reflected on the faces of his brother Junior, his sisters Sheila and Carmel, and other family members. There was little anyone could do to ease the pain. When Adrian finally passed, the room was filled with deep grief and sadness, but also with a sense of relief that he was no longer suffering.

His funeral services were held on October 9, 1993, in the Basilica of St. John the Baptist in St. John's. There was a capacity crowd in attendance, including many members of the legal profession, the judiciary, government, and a large number of people from the disability community for whom he had done so much. His brother-in-law Bob McGrath and his friend Ron Cole performed the readings. Premier Clyde Wells paid tribute to Adrian saying: "Throughout his life, Adrian demonstrated that the only barriers we face in life are the ones we set for ourselves. By his quiet efforts, he was able to improve the quality of life for disabled people." Adrian was buried close to his niece, Anne Marie Buckingham, at Holy Sepulchre Cemetery in St. John's, in a ceremony officiated by Father Molloy.

Maggie attended the funeral alongside the rest of the family, her presence commanding silent determination. As always, she remained stoic, her emotions carefully held in check, offering a steadying influence on those around her. Sometime later during a visit with her granddaughter Jeanine Battcock, the sensitive topic of Maggie's burial wishes arose. Though difficult to discuss, it was an important conversation. Maggie expressed her desire to be buried beside her son, Adrian, if possible, though she worried this might not be feasible due to space limitations at the cemetery.

Jeanine offered to investigate the situation and discovered that, due to an administrative error, the space next to Adrian had not been assigned. As a result, it was available for Maggie, allowing her wish to be fulfilled. In 1997, Maggie passed away at the age of 101, having outlived her son, Adrian, and her granddaughter, Anne Marie. Maggie's remarkable life was defined by her devotion to family and her profound faith. She was buried in Holy Sepulchre Cemetery next to Adrian.

On October 14, 1993, a tribute to Adrian was held in the Supreme Court of Newfoundland presided over by Chief Justice T. A. Hickman. Mr. Hickman noted that during his time working with Adrian, he grew to appreciate his sense of humour. He said, "Often on occasions, such as Christmas, I have fond memories of him entertaining us with his ability to manoeuvre, often at dangerous speeds, his wheelchair around the desks scattered throughout the Department much to the delight but apprehensions of all those in attendance." He went on to say:

> While Adrian was very loathe to take credit for any of his good work, I can say without fear of reasonable contradiction that he is responsible for the satisfactory transportation system now available to the handicapped of this community and that we

> are all indebted to Adrian Battcock for the inspiration he has given those who have had the good fortune to meet or work with him. While we are saddened by his death, we are grateful for the fact that Newfoundland has such justifiable pride in one of its native sons, Adrian G. Battcock.

On July 13, 1994, the Adrian Battcock Manor was officially opened in Grand Falls- Windsor. The facility was dedicated to the re-entry of disabled persons into the community. Battcock Manor is a sixteen-unit, partner-managed housing complex with Newfoundland and Labrador Housing Corporation. There are four two-bedroom units and twelve one-bedroom units, all of which are accessible and suitable for persons with mobility challenges. Residents organize their own social gatherings in the common lounge, and there is a large, beautiful backyard with plenty of space for gardening and gatherings. The YMCA provides building maintenance and assistance with lease requirements.

On November 4, 1994, the Ability Challenge Foundation Inc., a group incorporated to carry on Adrian's legacy and to assist persons with disabilities, held what became an annual art auction and dinner in his memory. The key address was given by Adrian's old friend, the Hon. Paul Dicks, Speaker of the Newfoundland Legislature. Over the years, the focus of the Ability Challenge Foundation shifted towards students with diverse disabilities. On November 25, 1994, a plaque in Adrian's memory was unveiled at City Hall in St. John's.

Adrian did not leave a will. His friend Ron Cole had offered to help with a will but Adrian said everything was in place. By not writing a will, everything would be left to his mother. He avoided any awkward situations that may have occurred with the intimate friends in his life. He believed this would ensure a smooth and conflict-free handling of his estate. This was so typical of Adrian. He wanted to keep everyone happy, always prioritizing the feelings and comfort of those around him and avoiding potential complications or conflicts. His natural inclination to avoid confrontation and make decisions that he thought would minimize distress for others was evident even in his decision not to leave a will.

Adrian's death at the age of fifty-eight marked the conclusion of an extraordinary journey that began in a small outport community in Newfoundland during the Great Depression years of the 1930s. His life had carried him far from those early days, through triumph and heartbreak. But as he lay dying, it was not his public achievements that came back to him most clearly. One memory stayed with him.

He was five years old, the summer before his life changed in ways he could not yet understand. He and Junior had gone trouting with their father at a small brook outside Brigus South. The day before, their father had dug worms and kept them in a tin. At the brook, he showed the boys how to put the worms on the hook and how to hold the fishing pole properly. Adrian remembered throwing his line into the water and feeling excited. Then, suddenly, he slipped and fell into the brook. The cold water shocked him. Right away, his father lifted him out and carried him home on his shoulders. What stayed with Adrian was not the fall or even the fishing trip itself, but the feeling of being carried—his father's strength and the sense of safety he felt in his arms.

Throughout his exceptional life, Adrian consistently put others before himself, dedicating his efforts to improving their lives. He remained ever mindful of the values his mother instilled in him, which guided his actions and decisions. Adrian cherished his family deeply and honoured their memory through his deeds and character. His life stands as a testament to his nieces and nephews of what truly defines a person. Through his steadfast love, selflessness, and dedication to justice and advocacy, Adrian exemplified the qualities of a genuinely compassionate and principled individual. His legacy serves as an enduring reminder of the impact one person can have on the lives of many, embodying the essence of character and integrity.

Eleanor Dawson, a graduate of Memorial University of Newfoundland, has been a leading voice in the province's cultural community for over forty years. Known for her creativity and vision, she has held production, administrative, and managerial roles that have shaped organizations, festivals, and cultural policy across Newfoundland and Labrador. Eleanor is also a traditional singer who has been an active participant in the folk culture of the province for the past fifty years, contributing to its preservation and celebration through performance and community engagement. After retiring from the provincial government in 2016, she embraced a new chapter as a freelance collaborator, working with community groups. Honoured with MusicNL's Industry Builder Award, she continues to inspire and support Newfoundland and Labrador's artistic landscape.

After a successful corporate career in Toronto, Jeanine (Jen) Battcock followed her heart to Newmarket, Ontario to be closer to her sister, Michele. There, she combined her two greatest passions—helping seniors and transforming homes—to build the successful Newfie Sisters Staging & Downsizing Inc. While Newmarket will always be home, a piece of Jen's heart will forever belong to Newfoundland. In her downtime, Jen can usually be found tending her woodland garden or spending time with the loves of her life: Jack and her son, Mark. As Adrian Battcock's niece, Jeanine was uniquely positioned to contribute to this biography, honouring her beloved uncle.